PLUTARCH

TEN FAMOUS LIVES

PLUTARCH
TEN FAMOUS LIVES

꧅꧅꧅꧅꧅꧅꧅꧅꧅꧅꧅꧅꧅꧅꧅꧅꧅꧅꧅꧅꧅꧅꧅꧅꧅꧅꧅꧅

THE DRYDEN TRANSLATION
REVISED BY ARTHUR HUGH CLOUGH

*Further Revised and Edited for Young Readers
and with an Introduction by*
CHARLES ALEXANDER ROBINSON, JR.

Plutarchus
=

E. P. DUTTON & CO., INC.,   NEW YORK

Published simultaneously in Canada by
Clarke, Irwin & Company Limited,
Toronto and Vancouver

Maps appearing in this book are adapted by Rafael
Palacios from maps drawn by Dr. Erwin Raisz for
Ancient History by C. A. Robinson, Jr.,
The Macmillan Company

Library of Congress Catalog Card Number: 62-14703

For Muriel S. Fine

CONTENTS

INTRODUCTION

Plutarch wrote his famous *Lives* of notable Greeks and Romans in Greek, for he was a Greek, born about 46 A.D. at Chaeronea. This was a little town of Boeotia, a district of central Greece. His birthplace was steeped in the kind of historical associations that must have made men think of the glorious past. Here, centuries earlier (in 338 B.C.), Philip II, King of Macedonia, and his son, Alexander, had brought to an end the freedom of the Greek city-states.

Greece is such a mountainous country that it was difficult for it to achieve political unity in early times. Greece was not a nation, not even a federation, until the Macedonian conquest. Earlier, during its greatest period, Greece was a collection of many city-states—independent political units situated in the valleys between the mountain ranges. They were passionately devoted to freedom, and each city-state felt that it should be completely sovereign in its domestic and foreign affairs. Some city-states, such as Athens, might build temporary empires, but the ideal of liberty always remained.

That ideal of liberty was seriously threatened by the Persian Empire when it attacked Greece proper (the Balkan Peninsula) at the very opening of the fifth century before Christ, Greece's most glorious century. Our book begins with this crisis in European civilization; and, through Plutarch's *Life of Themistocles,* we catch the drama of the day and the means by which the Greeks saved themselves.

The Greeks and others, such as the Egyptians and Syrians, looked upon the Persian Empire as practically equivalent to the civilized world. It was an immense Asiatic empire—much bigger than present-day Persia, or Iran—and it was very efficient and liberal in its rule; but it is also true that some people, at least, cannot develop under foreign domination. The Greeks of Asia Minor provide an example.

Asia Minor, which today is Turkey, had been the home of Greeks for centuries; the Greeks were not limited, as they now are, to the Balkan Peninsula and the islands of the Aegean Sea, but were settled around the Black and Mediterranean seas as well. When the Persian Empire conquered the ancient Greek city-states of Asia Minor, Greek civilization stopped developing in that part of the world. For one thing, the Greeks of Asia Minor now paid their taxes into the Persian treasury. Since the Persian government cared little for Greek art, the Greeks were no longer able to build temples, nor could they support sculptors and other artists. The joy of living, the satisfaction that comes from inquiring critically about the world and man's place in it, withered under foreign rule; consequently literature, no less than art, suffered.

Now our own civilization, through the medium of Rome, is based largely on the ancient Greek; it was vital for European culture that the Persian Empire should not spread from Asia Minor to Greece. Here is the importance of Themistocles. Year after year, as an elected Athenian official, Themistocles urged his fellow citizens to build a fleet. If the Athenians could defeat the Persians at sea, the Persian army would have to withdraw to Asia, because it would need a fleet to maintain its supplies in a land as poor as Greece. When the Greeks defeated the Persian fleet in the Bay of Salamis in 480 B.C., Themistocles was justly looked upon as the savior of Greece.

Fear of Persia remained, however, and that is why Athens was able to create a defensive alliance against the Persians. This alliance consisted chiefly of the Greek states along the Aegean coast of Asia Minor, and the islands—the very ones most exposed to possible Persian aggression. Under Pericles, the Athenians turned the alliance into a regular empire, although at home they created a wonderful democracy for themselves.

Democratic government was invented by the Greeks. The individual city-states varied in their constitutions, but the Athenian democracy, which was particularly successful, operated as follows. All free males over eighteen years of age met once every ten days in their assembly to decide the various questions involving their city and empire. We should note, in passing, the extraordinary education in government which the average Athenian received.

The questions put to the assembly had been discussed in advance by a Council of Five Hundred, whose members were chosen annually by lot. Here, again, was an excellent opportunity for a citizen to share in governmental responsibility, for the total population of Athens was only about a quarter of a million (this figure includes the children and others who lacked the suffrage: the women; the resident foreigners, who had settled down to do business; and the slaves, who were relatively few in number). A man might not have the luck of becoming a member of the council in his lifetime, but he certainly had a good chance of being one of the five thousand jurors selected each year. This right to be tried by your fellows was the very cornerstone of Athenian democracy, as indeed it is of any democracy.

At the top of the Athenian government stood the Board of Ten Generals—annually elected officials, who might be good generals or admirals, but who, in any case, were chosen for their executive ability. This was the office held for years by Pericles (as by Themistocles before him), and by his intellectual power and oratorical ability he persuaded his colleagues on the Board and the Athenians themselves to adopt his policies, as Plutarch's *Life of Pericles* makes clear.

Life at Athens under Pericles was full and vibrant; a wonderful freedom of speech went hand in hand with a willingness to try new ideas. The empire made the Athenians aware of a large world, while the increased

economic activities promoted prosperity. The tribute of
the empire was used to pay for various jobs; for instance,
it made possible the erection of beautiful buildings on
the Acropolis—Athens' sacred hill—which have been the
joy of mankind ever since. Ictinus, the architect of the
Parthenon, and Phidias, its sculptor, have won immortality. Democracy, with the opportunity it provides men
to develop themselves, brought all the arts, as well as
government itself, to an exceptionally high peak. There
now lived and worked in this small city the famous tragic
poets Aeschylus, Sophocles, and Euripides; the comic
poet Aristophanes; the historians Herodotus and Thucydides; the philosopher Socrates (his great pupil, Plato,
was born a decade after Pericles' death in 429 B.C.).
Rarely has civilization seen such a galaxy of brilliant men
at any one time.

Athena, the patron goddess of Athens, lived on Mt.
Olympus, so men said, with Zeus, Poseidon, and other
deities. Although they were a religious people, the Greeks
nevertheless placed their chief faith in the ability of men
to conduct their own affairs. As Protagoras put it, "Man
is the measure of all things." If we except the innate
ability of the Greeks (which defies explanation), it was
this faith in man himself which probably best accounts
for the magnificent flowering of the mind and spirit in
Periclean Athens.

Athens, however, had a dread enemy in southern
Greece, in the Peloponnesus, as it is called. This was

Sparta; and, in 431 B.C., the two antagonists began the long and terrible Peloponnesian War, which ended only with the defeat of Athens in 404 B.C. Toward the beginning of the war, Pericles lost his life in an awful plague that carried off perhaps a fourth of Athens' population. The war might have ended fairly soon, at least in a stalemate, had it not been for the ambitions of Alcibiades, a kinsman of Pericles. In his *Life of Alcibiades*, Plutarch vividly presents this brilliant, and yet contemptible, man.

With all their marvelous creative contributions to civilization, the Greeks made one very special mistake: they were unwilling to surrender the sovereignty, or autonomy, of their city-states to a wider union, such as federation. The necessity of finding the greater military strength, which union would give, became imperative as the power of Macedonia increased. The Macedonian Kingdom was located in the mountains along the northern fringe of Greece; the Macedonians themselves were a branch of the Greek people, speaking a Greek dialect, but unlike the Greeks southward, they formed a compact, vigorous nation. Civilization had come rather late to the Macedonians, and many Greeks looked upon them as practically barbarians. One Athenian in particular, Demosthenes, feared the Macedonian king, Philip. In his *Life of Demosthenes*, Plutarch shows how the greatest of Greek orators—by the sheer force of his oratory, for he held no office—stood for the freedom of the city-states against Philip. But Philip's fine professional army prevailed, and at Chaeronea, in 338 B.C., the Greeks were conquered, as we said at the opening of our introductory remarks.

First under Philip, and then under his famous son, Alexander the Great, the Greeks were united in a federation. It was then that Alexander set off with his Macedonians and Greek allies to punish the Persians—as the war cry had it—for their invasion of Greece in the previous century. It is well known that Alexander conquered everywhere he went, but it is not so well known that he evolved a dream of universalism, of co-operation between peoples, something we might describe as a dream of the brotherhood of man.

Plutarch, in his *Life of Alexander,* brings this out. Indeed, Alexander's new idea for mankind was picked up by others and eventually was magnificently expressed by St. Paul, a contemporary of Plutarch, in his great dream of a world in which there shall be neither Greek nor Jew, barbarian nor Scythian, bond nor free. In that dream, we might add, lies antiquity's challenge to all posterity.

The birthplace of Plutarch, we have suggested, was important, for as he walked around Chaeronea he was bound to reflect on the glory and freedom of classical Greece. The date of his birth (approximately 46 A.D.) is also important, because by that time Greece had not only long since ceased to be free but was a province belonging to the Roman Empire.

It had come about in this manner. The world that Alexander conquered broke up after his death (323 B.C.) into large kingdoms. Part of Alexander's significance is that he put an end to city-state democracy and substituted in its place the large monarchical state. These states were chiefly the Seleucid Kingdom in Asia—named after Alexander's general, Seleucus—and the Ptolemaic Kingdom in Egypt, named after Alexander's general, Ptolemy. That is to say, the world that Alexander conquered was ruled after his death by his Macedonian successors. Their rule continued for three centuries, until Rome gradually absorbed their kingdoms. Cleopatra, for example, was a Macedonian, the last of the Ptolemies, and when Rome defeated her and Antony, her Kingdom of Egypt fell into Rome's lap and completed the Roman conquest of the Mediterranean.

During the three centuries when Alexander's successors reigned, the world very largely adopted Hellenism, Greek civilization, as a common culture. That explains why the *New Testament* was ultimately written in Greek —and not in Hebrew, as had been the *Old Testament* —for Jesus' Apostles wished to carry their message to all.

It was this world of the East, combined with Gaul and Britain in the West, that Rome eventually conquered and incorporated in its extraordinary universal state. The Romans, of course, had their own long history, but by 509 B.C. the last kings had been driven out—by, among others, an ancestor of that Brutus who was to murder

Julius Caesar. The Republic was now established. The Roman Republic created at least a potential democracy, and it also conquered an empire.

But, in 218 B.C., Hannibal invaded Italy. He came from Carthage, which the ancient Semitic city of Phoenician Tyre had founded in North Africa about 800 B.C. With Alexander and Caesar, Hannibal ranks as one of the three greatest military geniuses of antiquity. Plutarch's *Life of Fabius* shows us just how close Hannibal came to winning. Then, in his *Life of Cato the Elder*, Plutarch portrays a stiff-necked, Roman conservative, who attempted to resist the Greek and other foreign influences which threatened to inundate Rome after its momentous victory over Hannibal.

All kinds of problems, as a matter of fact, now faced the Roman Republic, chief among them the striving for personal dominion. The last century of the Roman Republic witnessed a veritable revolution—a series of civil wars and terrible proscriptions—as one general after another tried to seize the government for himself. Plutarch's *Life of Julius Caesar* tells us about the most extraordinary of these men, while his *Life of Cicero* shows how one great man stood by the Republic and the cause of freedom.

On the Ides of March, March 15, 44 B.C., Caesar was murdered. Who was to succeed him? Was it to be his friend Mark Antony, with Cleopatra, or his grand-nephew Octavian? The whole story is dramatically unfolded by Plutarch in his *Life of Antony*. Octavian's victory over Antony in 31 B.C. at the naval battle of Actium, off the northwestern coast of Greece, was followed by the suicides of Antony and Cleopatra in Alexandria; this was the Egyptian capital, which had been founded by Alexander and was named after him. The Roman Republic and its century of civil wars were now finished. The Roman Empire, in the formal sense of having emperors, began.

Octavian, under the name of Augustus, became Rome's first emperor. He ruled a long time and well, and was followed by Tiberius and Caligula. In the reign of the fourth emperor, Claudius, Plutarch was born. He lived through the reign of Nero and well into the most glorious period of Roman imperial history. Edward Gibbon, in his famous *Decline and Fall of the Roman Empire,* calls it "without hesitation the most happy and prosperous period in the history of the world." It was during this time—in the reign of the emperor Hadrian, about 120 A.D.—that Plutarch died. He was perhaps seventy-five years old.

It is abundantly clear that Plutarch is an important historical source. Actually, Shakespeare got almost all his knowledge of ancient history—of Caesar and Antony, for example—from Sir Thomas North's translation of a French version of Plutarch by Jacques Amyot. We ourselves, with our tremendous accumulation of archaeological knowledge, to say nothing of all the ancient literary works at our disposal, do not find Plutarch quite so indispensable. Nevertheless, we are grateful to him for good historical writing, often at its most exciting best.

This is because Plutarch chose to cast his historical thinking in the form of biographies of important people, people who counted in some extraordinary way or other in the development of human affairs. He turned biographical writing into a regular category, or genre, of literature, and so it has remained ever since. The over-all scheme of his *Parallel Lives,* as he called his biographies, was to pair a famous Greek and a famous Roman and follow it up with a comparison of the two; the *Lives* of Alexander and Caesar, for example, although his comparison of these two great generals has been lost.

Plutarch greatly admired Rome's world state, which at long last had brought wars to an end. Indeed, the amazing Roman Peace and its widespread prosperity lasted more than a quarter of a millennium from the accession of Augustus; and after the Peace had ended, it took several centuries more for the Roman Empire to die and to break up into the great states, such as Italy and France, which comprise modern Europe.

But Plutarch, of course, was a Greek, who wished to interpret his people and their history to the Roman conqueror. This was a strong motive in the composition of his biographies. Finally, we must say that Plutarch had another and very deep purpose in his writing, for at heart he was a moralist and hoped to educate his readers by presenting the example and warning of the famous men of the past.

Although Plutarch wrote many essays in addition to his biographies, he also found time to serve as a magistrate at Chaeronea and in various other official capacities, especially under the Roman emperor Trajan. His official work and studies brought him to Rome during the course of his travels. He was happy with his wife and children, but not much more is known concerning him personally. His immortality rests on his literary skill. The Oxford University Press has published an admirable book by Gilbert Highet entitled *The Classical Tradition;* it interprets ancient authors, Plutarch among them, and shows their influence on later centuries.

My choice of these particular biographies has been determined by the importance of the individuals themselves and by the innate interest with which Plutarch has clothed them. Even so, much (including matters of purely antiquarian value) has been omitted from each biography. The Greek *Lives* come first, and then the Roman, a chronological order being maintained within each group, so that the sweep of history is brought out. The greatest period of ancient Greek history begins with the Persian Wars and Themistocles, and it ends with Alexander. The great drama of the Roman Republic begins with Fabius and the others who opposed Hannibal, and with Antony the Republic came to an end.

The audience of this book is the younger reader; eventually, as college student or layman, he will wish to turn to Plutarch again and read *in toto* these biographies, and others of the fifty that survive, not only for their content but also for a fuller appreciation of Plutarch's genius. At any rate, it is my hope that this presentation of what may fairly be claimed as the cream of Plutarch will so inspire him. In this book, meanwhile, he will indeed come into close contact with some of the most decisive events and ideas in ancient Greek and Roman history, as highlighted by famous individuals and as presented by one of the world's most celebrated biographers.

I do not imagine that many persons will read this book through at one sitting, and consequently it has occurred to me that it might be helpful if I repeated—either within the text itself or in the parenthetical paragraph with which I introduce each biography—an occasional background fact; for example, that one Greek talent equals approximately $1,800. I have thoroughly revised and at times rewritten the Dryden-Clough translation of Plutarch. My wife has, as always, helped me greatly in the preparation of this book. She and I together offer the volume in appreciation to Mrs. Fine for a long and valued Classical association.

C. A. ROBINSON, JR.

PROVIDENCE, RHODE ISLAND

PLUTARCH
TEN FAMOUS LIVES

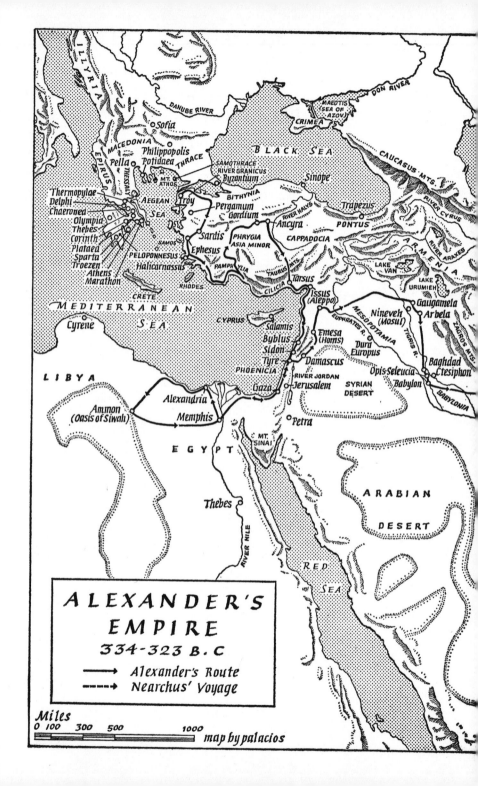

ALEXANDER'S EMPIRE

334-323 B.C

→ Alexander's Route

----→ Nearchus' Voyage

Miles

0 100 300 500 1000

map by palacios

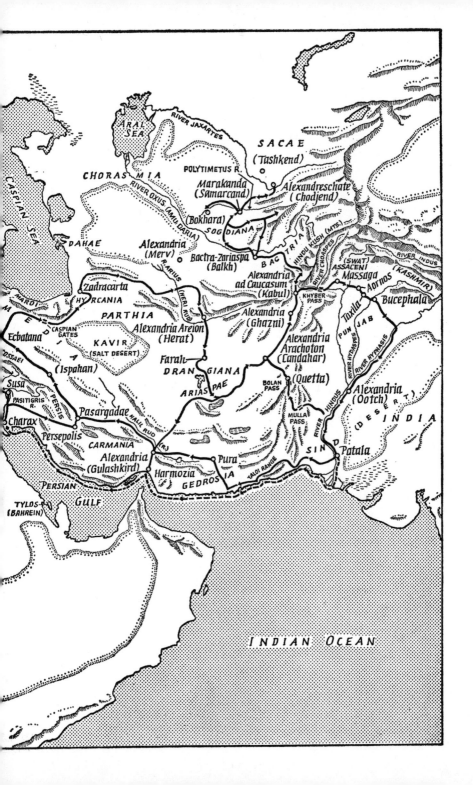

THEMISTOCLES

*(Born in the latter part of the sixth century B.C.; died
ca. 460 B.C. The great classical century of Greece—the
fifth before Christ—opened with invasions by the Persian Empire, which stretched in all its might from European Thrace to India. In 492 B.C. a Persian fleet was
wrecked at Mt. Athos, a peninsula projecting into the
northern Aegean Sea; the Persian army had to return
to Asia, for, without the navy to supply it, a large force
could not maintain itself in Greece. In 490 B.C., at Marathon, Athens defeated a much smaller Persian contingent, which sailed directly from Asia Minor. As another
invasion threatened, political strife increased at Athens.
Themistocles, on the basis of the experience in 492 B.C.,
urged the Athenians to build a large fleet, win at sea,
and thus compel the Persian army to withdraw. In 480
B.C. the Persians, following the land and sea route of a
dozen years earlier, overwhelmed the Spartans at the
Pass of Thermopylae; there was an indecisive naval conflict off the nearby island of Euboea, at Artemisium; but
in the Bay of Salamis, within sight of burning Athens,
the Greeks destroyed the Persian fleet. It may be fairly
claimed that Themistocles' strategy saved European civilization from Oriental conquest. Next year the battle of
Plataea brought the Persian Wars to an end; the Athenian*

5

Empire, which Pericles later guided, was born from the
need of possible defense against further Persian aggres-
sion.)

The birth of Themistocles was too obscure to do him
honor, for his father, Neocles, was not a distinguished Athenian, and his mother came from Thrace.
Themistocles always had a vehement disposition and was
ever eager for action. His school holidays were spent in-
venting orations—generally accusing or excusing his companions of something—until finally his teacher said to
him, "My boy, someday you will be great—whether
for good or evil I don't know." Moreover, Themistocles
was very careless about his lessons in manners and seemed
eager to know only how to manage affairs. Later on, when
he was in the company of people who engaged in what
are commonly known as the liberal and elegant amuse-
ments, he would readily admit that he could not play
a stringed instrument. "But," he would arrogantly add,
"give me a city, no matter how small and obscure, and
I will make it great and glorious."

Themistocles was not happy as a boy, for he was in-
clined merely to follow his own feelings without control-
ling them by reason. And he used to say himself that the
wildest colts make the best horses, if only they get properly broken in. But since he passionately desired to win
first place in public affairs, he was willing to accept the

hatred of the most powerful leaders of Athens. In particular, he was opposed by Aristides. Aristides was mild in nature and always put the interest of the state before any personal popularity. The innovations which Themistocles proposed often struck him as dangerous to the state.

Themistocles was so carried away by dreams of glory that, even though he was still young at the time the battle was fought against the Persians at Marathon, he would remain quiet whenever anyone spoke of Miltiades, the victorious Athenian general of that day. And when people asked him why he was avoiding his usual places of recreation, he replied that the thought of Miltiades' trophy kept him awake at night.

Some people said the battle of Marathon had brought the war with Persia to an end. Themistocles, however, saw that it was simply the beginning of far greater conflicts and, fortunately for all Greece, he prepared himself and his city as best he could. First of all, he persuaded the Athenians to devote the revenues from the state silver mines at Laurium to the building of a large fleet. Next, to further the success of his program, he brought about the exile of Aristides. At this time various messengers from Xerxes, the Great King of Persia, were going around Greece demanding earth and water as a sign of submission. Themistocles seized their interpreter and put him to death for daring to announce the Persian demands in the Greek language.

When Xerxes, with his vast host, invaded northern Greece, the allied Greek fleet was sent to guard the straits of Artemisium. To insure harmony among the Athenian and Spartan contingents, Themistocles said that Eurybiades, the Spartan, should be the chief admiral. The size of the Persian armada frightened Eurybiades, however, and he determined to withdraw to southern Greece, to the Peloponnesus. Herodotus, the historian, says that Themistocles had to bribe him to make him stay.

The skirmishes between the Greeks and Persians at Artemisium were not in themselves important, and yet the Greeks gained good experience from them. By actual trial in the midst of danger, they found out that neither number of ships, nor rich decorations, nor boastful shouts, nor barbarous songs of victory could be terrifying to men who knew how to fight. For the first step toward victory is courage.

Then came the news of Thermopylae, that Leonidas, the Spartan king, and all his men had been slain and that Xerxes was master on land. The Greek fleet, accordingly, withdrew southward.

As Xerxes continued his march, he burned the Greek cities and countryside. It was obvious that the Athenians would have to abandon their city, while there was still time, but they hated to do it. Themistocles did all that he could to make them change their minds. The sacred serpent of Athena disappeared from its temple; at the suggestion of Themistocles, the priest announced that

the goddess had left the city for the sea. And then Themistocles reminded the Athenians of the oracle of Del-
phi, which said that they should trust their walls of wood;
the walls of wood, he explained, could mean nothing but
their ships.

Finally his opinion prevailed, and it was decreed that
the city should be abandoned to the protection of Athena,
the patron goddess of Athens. Most Athenians sent their
parents, wives, children, and slaves to Troezen, on the
opposite Peloponnesian coast, a spectacle that stirred both
admiration and pity. Those who were able to bear arms
embarked for the nearby island of Salamis. Themistocles
further showed his greatness of character by recalling
Aristides from exile, in order that the entire state might
be unified in the crisis.

Eurybiades, the Spartan, was still admiral of the allied Greek fleet, but he was timid in the face of danger
and thought that they should retire to the Isthmus of
Corinth; a wall had been built across this narrow stretch
of land, and the Greek army had been stationed there to
keep the Persians out of the Peloponnesus. Themistocles
opposed retreat, whereupon Eurybiades tried to check his
impatience by pointing out that runners at the Olympic
Games who started before the others were lashed. "And,"
Themistocles replied, "those that are left behind don't
win the crown."

Nevertheless, Eurybiades and the other Spartans began to think once again of retreating, when the Persian

fleet arrived off Athens at the harbor of Phaleron. And their hearts sank further as Xerxes and his army camped on the coast. Themistocles, of course, did not want to lose their present great advantage; the narrow strait between the island of Salamis and the mainland gave the small Greek fleet a real chance, for the Persians would not have the necessary space in which to maneuver their huge armada. And so Themistocles thought of this trick. He sent his trusted slave to Xerxes with orders to tell him that Themistocles, the Athenian admiral, now favored the Persian side and was about to flee, and that the Persians, by sending some of their fleet around the island of Salamis and blocking up the exit, could destroy the Greeks.

Xerxes believed the message and was overjoyed. He ordered his admirals to close all avenues of escape and then went himself to the beach and sat on a golden throne, with secretaries round about him to write down everything that happened in the fight.

The news that the Persians had surrounded the island of Salamis with their ships forced the Spartans to fight. The tragic poet Aeschylus, in his play *The Persians*, says that the enemy had 1,000 ships. The Athenians had 180, with eighteen marines on each ship, four of them archers and the rest regular infantrymen. Just as Themistocles had selected the most advantageous place for the battle, so now he chose the best time for fighting. He waited till the moment when a fresh breeze blew in from the open sea, which would create a swell in the narrow channel. This would not trouble the low-lying Greek ships, which stood only a little above the water, but it would slow down the heavy, cumbersome Persian boats with their high sterns and lofty decks. Thus the Greeks would be able to maneuver quickly and ram the Persians amidships.

And that is the way it turned out. The Persians had to fight in the narrow strait and could use only a part of their fleet. Moreover, their ships got mixed up with one another. The Greeks charged them all day until evening when, as the poet Simonides says, they won the most glorious victory in history. Their courage did it, but the actual victory had been made possible by the wisdom of Themistocles.

Themistocles now went to Aristides and suggested that they sail to the Hellespont and destroy the pontoon bridge, thus leaving the Persians stranded in Europe. But Aristides said they should desire nothing more than to have the Persians hurry themselves back into Asia, and that if there were not already a bridge across the Hellespont, they should build one if they could. Accordingly, Themistocles sent another false message to Xerxes, saying that the Greeks intended to destroy his bridge. Full of anger and fear, Xerxes withdrew from Greece, but he left behind a force under Mardonius to spend the winter there. The Greeks annihilated it the following year at Plataea.

Herodotus says that Aegina, of all the cities in Greece, fought best at the battle of Salamis. As for the various generals, when they voted on the best commander, each man gave first vote to himself and second to Themistocles. At the next Olympic Games, just as soon as Themistocles entered, the spectators took no further notice of the contestants, but spent the day applauding him and pointing him out to strangers. Themistocles confessed to his friends that this rewarded him for all his labors on behalf of the Greeks.

All kinds of anecdotes are told about Themistocles and his great love of honor. For example, when he was the Athenian admiral, he would never attend to isolated business, but would let it accumulate till the day before sailing, to give an appearance of his importance and power. And he used to say that the Athenians did not really honor or admire him, but used him like a sort of plane tree; they would shelter themselves under him in bad weather, but as soon as it was fine again, they would pick his leaves and cut his branches. One day he laughed at his son, who managed to get his mother, and through her his father, to indulge him. "My boy," he said, "you have the most power in Greece. For the Athenians command the rest of Greece, I command the Athenians, your mother commands me, and you command her." Of two men who were in love with his daughter, he said that he preferred the man of worth to the one who was rich, for he desired a man without riches more than riches without a man. This gives an idea of his sayings.

The Spartans, of course, were anxious for the Athenians not to rebuild their fortification walls after the destruction of their city. Accordingly, Themistocles went down to Sparta and asserted that the Athenians had no such intentions. He kept the Spartans discussing the matter with him long enough for the Athenians, without any interference, to rebuild their walls. Next, Themistocles established Piraeus as the special harbor of Athens, for it had the best natural advantages. It was this act which really tied city and port together and made the people throw in their lot, so to speak, with the sea rather than the land. This increased the authority of the people against the aristocrats, for power fell more and more into the hands of the sailors. It was generally believed that the Athenian maritime empire had its origin in the development of democracy in the city.

Hence Themistocles incurred the displeasure of the oligarchical Spartans, who now favored the Athenian aristocrat Cimon and hoped that he would crush Themistocles. As for the Athenians, they listened with increasing frequency to various charges brought against Themistocles, until at last they were convinced that he was intriguing with the Persians and exiled him.

Themistocles now took up his residence at Argos and other places in Greece and then, with considerable misgivings, he fled to Persia. To his surprise, the Great King received him with kindness and allowed him to live in comfort within the empire. Eventually, however, he committed suicide at Magnesia, a city in Asia Minor. He was sixty-five years old.

Today, when you enter the harbor of Piraeus, just at the place where a neck of land projects into the sea, you can see the tomb of Themistocles, which the Athenians in their shame built in his honor. The tomb looks right down on the merchants and their ships as they come and go.

PERICLES

(ca. 495–429 B.C. Leader of the Athenian democracy and creator of the Age which bears his name. It was now that the Parthenon and other beautiful buildings were built on the Acropolis and elsewhere; Sophocles and others wrote their great plays. The Athenian Empire under Pericles' direction, however, came into conflict with Sparta. Pericles died near the beginning of the ensuing Peloponnesian War—431–404 B.C.—which Athens ultimately lost.)

Pericles was of the noblest birth, both on his father's side and his mother's. Xanthippus, his father, defeated the fleet of the Persian king at Mycale. He was the husband of Agariste, the niece of Cleisthenes, the famous democratic reformer at Athens. Just before Pericles was born, his mother dreamed that she had given birth to a lion. As a matter of fact, Pericles was perfectly formed in all respects, except that his head was longish and out of proportion. For this reason artists made paintings and statues of him wearing a helmet, but nevertheless the comic poets, in their hard-hitting fashion, called him squill-head.

Pericles was fortunate in his teachers. Damonides taught him music, and Zeno natural philosophy. But the person who gave Pericles his sublimity of purpose and character was Anaxagoras, who came from Clazomenae in Asia Minor. Men of that day called Anaxagoras Nous —that is to say, Mind or Intelligence—in admiration of his knowledge of nature and also because he was the first philosopher who did not ascribe the formation of the world to accident but rather to unadulterated intelligence. For this man Pericles had the highest esteem; he got from him not only dignity of language, far above the buffooneries of mob oratory, but also a certain composure of countenance. His serenity and calmness, the even tone of his voice, these he learned from Anaxagoras, and they had the greatest effect on his hearers. Moreover, Anaxagoras freed Pericles' mind of superstition and the ignorant fear of eclipses and other appearances in the heavens.

When he entered politics, Pericles sided not with the rich and few, but with the many and poor. One reason for this was that his chief rival, Cimon, led the aristocratic faction, and Pericles thought that the party of the people gave him a better chance to secure power. Once embarked on a political career, he immediately adopted a new course of life and arrangement of his time. For example, he was never seen to walk in any street except that which led to the market place and council hall. He refused invitations of friends to supper and all visiting of that kind.

The point is, these friendly meetings quickly defeat any assumed superiority, and it is difficult to maintain an expression of gravity. And to avoid having the common people become too accustomed to him, he spoke to them but rarely, and then only on great occasions. He was so superior to all others in the art of speaking that he was given the nickname of "the Olympian." The comic poets of the day refer to Pericles' "thundering and lightning" when he harangued the people, and of his wielding a dreadful thunderbolt in his tongue.

Thucydides, the great contemporary historian, describes the rule of Pericles as an aristocratic government that went by the name of a democracy, but was in fact the supremacy of a single great man. Others, however, say that the people were first led by Pericles to all manner of evils, such as the appropriations of subject territory, allowances for attending the theater, and payments for performing public duties. These bad habits, they say, changed the Athenians from a sober, thrifty people, who maintained themselves by their own labors, to lovers of expense, intemperance, and license.

At any rate, it was Pericles who constructed the public and sacred buildings that chiefly adorned the city of Athens and evoked in strangers the greatest admiration and even astonishment. Today, of course, they are the only proof of Greece's ancient power and wealth. And yet, of all Pericles' actions that his enemies attacked, it was his building program that produced the severest criticism. They said that Athens had lost its good reputation by moving the common treasury of the Greeks from the island of Delos to Athens itself, on the pretext that the Persians might seize it. And now Pericles, they continued, was taking the money and adorning Athens like a vain woman, draping around her neck precious stones and statues and temples. Pericles, on the other hand, told the Athenians that they did not need to give their allies in the empire any account of the money, as long as they defended them from Persia.

The materials used in these public works, and the men needed for the labor, were so many and so varied that almost everyone in the state prospered as a result. Then, as the works rose from their foundations, they were no less stately in size than exquisite in form. The artisans strove to excel the material and the design with the beauty of their own workmanship, and yet the most wonderful thing of all was the rapidity of their execution. Some people thought that it would take several generations to complete them, and yet they were done in the height of one man's political service. They say that Zeuxis once heard another painter boast of his speed and arrogantly replied, "I take a long time." It is true that ease and speed do not necessarily give a work lasting solidity or exactness of beauty; a man must be given time to create. Therefore, Pericles' works are to be especially admired, for they were made quickly and have lasted long. Each piece of work, when completed, looked beautiful and elegant, and today they are so vigorous and fresh that they still look as if they had just been made.

Phidias, the great sculptor, was the general artistic superintendent. Callicrates and Ictinus were the architects of the Parthenon. The Propylaea, or entrances to the Acropolis, were finished in five years' time; Mnesicles was the principal architect. And many other buildings were erected at this time, such as the Odeon or music hall and, at Eleusis, the Hall of the Mysteries.

Pericles eventually was able to put down the political opposition to himself. He brought unity to the city and got all the affairs of the Athenians into his own hands, the imperial tribute as well as the army and navy, and extended Athens' power, over other Greeks in part and in part over barbarians [non-Greeks]. After this, he was no longer the same man he had been before. He was not so gentle and familiar with the populace as formerly, nor would he yield to their pleasures and whims. His rule was austerely aristocratic, and he employed it for his country's best interests. Generally he was able to lead the people along by their own consent, by persuading them what was to be done; but occasionally he had to force them against their will to do what was for their advantage.

The source of Pericles' predominance was not only his power of language but, as Thucydides states, the reputation of his life and the confidence that all felt in his character. He was free from every kind of corruption and superior to all temptations of money. As a matter of fact, he did not increase his paternal inheritance by a drachma.

In his military conduct, Pericles gained a reputation for wariness. He would not engage in a battle that seemed uncertain, nor did he envy the glory of generals whose rash adventures sometimes met with brilliant success. Rather, he used to say to the Athenians that, as far as it lay in his power, they would live forever. Therefore he curbed their passion for foreign conquest and directed their strength chiefly to securing what they already had. He supposed that it would be quite enough if they kept the Lacedaemonians, or Spartans, in check.

Since his expedition against the island of Samos was thought by some to have been undertaken to please Aspasia, this might be a good place to inquire about the woman. What art or charming quality did she have that enabled her to captivate the greatest statesmen and caused philosophers to speak about her, not always to her disparagement, either? It is acknowledged that she was born at Miletus in Asia Minor. And they say that she made her advances to men of great power in imitation of Thargelia, a courtesan of Asia Minor. Thargelia was a real beauty, charming and wise. Among her many suitors were Greeks, and all these she brought over to the Persian side, and thus she sowed discord among the Greek cities of Asia Minor. So, according to some, Pericles courted Aspasia on account of her skill in politics. Even

Socrates occasionally visited her; and men would bring their wives with them to listen to her. But probably Pericles' chief feeling for her sprang from the passion of love. He already had a wife, a relative of his, and they had two sons. But they did not agree very well and decided to part; she married another man, and Pericles took Aspasia. He loved her with wonderful affection and every day, as he went to and from the market place, he saluted her with a kiss.

After the reduction of Samos, Pericles returned to Athens and took care that those who had died in the war should be honorably buried. He also made a funeral oration in their honor, as was the custom, and for this he was greatly admired. When he came down from the speaker's platform, many women complimented him and crowned him with garlands, like a victorious athlete. Some persons, however, said that Agamemnon, the leader of the Greeks before Troy, had taken ten years to conquer a barbarous city; whereas Pericles, in nine months, had reduced a great Greek city. But Thucydides tells us that Pericles deserved the glory of the victory, because the issue of the war was uncertain and it was possible that the Samians might have wrested the dominion of the sea from Athenian hands.

There are those who maintain that Pericles—by the policies he adopted toward Corinth, Megara, and other allies of Sparta—was the cause of the Peloponnesian War. When, on the outbreak of the war, the Spartans and their allies invaded Attica, Pericles withdrew the population from the countryside into the city. He did not feel that Athens had the manpower to fight on land as well as sea; and the fleet had to be maintained for the importation of food. To those who urged going out to fight, he said, "The olive trees that are cut down will grow up again in a short time, but men, once lost, cannot easily be recovered." So he shut the city gates, placed guards everywhere for security, and trusted his own judgment against those who angrily protested his management of the war. His plan, which he now put into effect, was to send the Athenian fleet around the Peloponnesus, ravaging the country and plundering the cities. Consequently, although the Peloponnesians did the Athenians much harm by land, they suffered greatly themselves from the attacks by sea. In fact, the war would have quickly ended, as Pericles prophesied, had not some divine power intervened.

This was the terrible plague which fell upon the city and carried off the young in their prime as well as the old. People were enraged at Pericles. They said that the plague had been caused by the country population coming into the city, where they lived in the summer heat crowded together in hovels. The Athenians, therefore, now deprived Pericles of his office and fined him.

Pericles lost his sister and most of his relatives and friends and advisers in the plague. However, on these occasions he did not give up his high spirit and the greatness of his mind, nor was he seen ever to weep at a funeral, until the death of his only remaining legitimate son.

The Athenians, after they had tried out other generals for the war and had listened to other men speak on public affairs, regretted the loss of Pericles and invited him to resume his office of general. But he stayed at home in mourning, until finally Alcibiades and other friends persuaded him to appear before the people. And then, when they had made him general again, he accepted.

It was at this time that the plague seized Pericles himself, not with sharp and violent fits, as it did others, but with a dull and lingering distemper. Little by little it wasted the strength of his body. When he was near the end, the best of the citizens and those of his friends who were still alive came to see him. They sat down beside him and spoke of his great merit and of his power. Then they enumerated his famous actions and the number of his victories. And thus they continued to talk among themselves, as if Pericles could not understand them and had lost consciousness. But he had listened all the while. At last he spoke up and said that he was amazed that they should commend him for things that were due to luck and had happened to many other generals, but had failed to mention the most important thing of all. "For," he said, "no Athenian has ever put on mourning because of me."

Pericles deserves our high admiration, not only for his mild and even temper, which he maintained through the struggles of his life; but also because of his high spirit which insisted that, in the exercise of his immense power, he should never be envious nor mistreat an opponent. To me it appears that so unblemished a life, at the height of power and position, may well be called Olympian, in accordance with our conceptions of the divine beings to whom, as the authors of everything good and nothing evil, we ascribe the rule and government of the world.

The course of public affairs at Athens after his death produced a quick sense of the loss of Pericles. Those who resented his authority while he lived, because it eclipsed their own, now had to put up with other orators and demagogues. They readily acknowledged that there had never been a disposition as moderate and reasonable as his. His power, which formerly they called by the name of monarchy and tyranny, now appeared to have been the chief bulwark of the public safety. During his life he restrained the flood of mischief and vice that overwhelmed the city after his death.

ALCIBIADES

(ca. 450–404 B.C. After the Peloponnesian War had been raging ten years, a wealthy Athenian aristocrat, named Nicias, arranged the peace that bears his name. This was in 421 B.C. The next years, however, were constantly disturbed by the ambitions of Alcibiades, the nephew and ward of Pericles, a brilliant but self-seeking individual.)

Alcibiades is supposed to have been descended from Ajax, the hero in the Trojan War. At any rate, his father fought well in the naval battle against the Persians at Artemisium, and his mother belonged to the noble Alcmaeonid family, as did Pericles. Much of Alcibiades' fame came from the friendship that Socrates, the philosopher, had for him.

Perhaps it is immaterial to say anything about the physical handsomeness of Alcibiades, except to note that it bloomed in his infancy, in his youth, and in his manhood. Even the lisp which he had gave a certain persuasiveness to his speech. The inconsistencies in the conduct of his life varied with his fortunes, but his strongest characteristic was probably his ambition and desire to be superior. A good many anecdotes are told about him which bear this out. For example, as a youth he was wrestling and was afraid that he might be thrown. Accordingly, he got the hand of his antagonist into his mouth and bit it as hard as he could. The other boy let go of him and said, "You bite just like a woman, Alcibiades." "No," he replied, "like a lion."

When Alcibiades began his studies, he obeyed his teachers pretty well, but he refused to play the flute. He said it was a sordid thing, disfiguring the face, whereas if one played the lute or lyre he could sing at the same time. One consequence of this was that playing the flute soon ceased to be one of the liberal accomplishments among the Athenians.

It is true that some aristocratic persons sought Alcibiades' company merely because of his physical charm. But Socrates was able to detect his natural and noble qualities underneath. He feared, however, that Alcibiades might be corrupted by all the attention he received, by the flatterers who visited him, and by what we vulgarly call the material things that surrounded him. On his side, Alcibiades was able to discern the true worth of Socrates. So they grew intimate, and Alcibiades now listened to language that was free of hollow flattery.

While he was still quite young, Alcibiades was a soldier in the expedition against Potidaea in northern Greece. He and Socrates tented together and stood next to each other in battle. In one sharp skirmish, Alcibiades was wounded and would have been killed, had not Socrates thrown himself in front of him and saved him.

In another battle, when the Athenians were routed, Socrates was retreating on foot, but Alcibiades, who was on horseback, stayed to protect him even though the enemy were pressing hard.

Once Alcibiades boxed Hipponicus on the ear. This man was the father of Callias, who became the richest person in Athens. Alcibiades had no reason to hit him, but did it as a joke. When news of this spread through Athens, people were offended by his insolence. Early the next morning, therefore, Alcibiades went to the house of Hipponicus, took off his clothes and told him to scourge him as he pleased. This caused Hipponicus to forget his resentment and, in fact, not much later he gave Alcibiades his daughter Hipparete in marriage.

Hipparete was a dutiful wife, but eventually she tired of her husband's continual entertainment of courtesans, foreigners as well as Athenians, and retired to her brother's house. This did not seem to bother Alcibiades, and he continued to live in the same luxury as before. But when Hipparete sought a formal divorce, he seized her in the courthouse, picked her up, and carried her home. She continued to live with him till her death, which occurred not long afterward.

Alcibiades had a large and handsome dog which cost him 70 minas [1 mina = $30]. The dog's principal ornament was his tail, but Alcibiades had it cut off. When his friends exclaimed at this and said that all Athens was sorry for the dog and condemned his action, he laughed and said, "That's just what I wanted to happen. I wanted the Athenians to talk about this, so that they wouldn't have something worse to say about me."

Alcibiades had many great advantages for entering public life: his noble birth, his riches, his personal courage in battle, and his multitude of friends and dependents. But he would not let his power with the people rest on anything except his gift of eloquence. The comic poets admit that he was a master in the art of speaking. However, we must bear in mind that he had the highest capacity for discerning what was the right thing to say.

Alcibiades spent large sums of money on his horses and chariots. No other private person, or even a king, ever sent seven chariots to the Olympic Games. And once he had the extraordinary distinction of winning the first, second, and fourth prizes at Olympia.

Alcibiades was disturbed by the honors that Nicias gained among the enemies of Athens, as well as by those that the Athenians heaped upon him. Nicias was a rich Athenian noble and an accomplished general. It was commonly said in Greece that the Peloponnesian War had been begun by Pericles and then brought to a halt by Nicias, and the peace was generally called the Peace of Nicias. Alcibiades was extremely annoyed at this and full of envy, and set himself to break the treaty. He disturbed affairs at Argos and elsewhere, got himself elected general at Athens, and whittled away Nicias' prestige.

With his good deeds, his sagacity and eloquence, Alcibiades mingled exorbitant luxury and wantonness in his eating and drinking and dissolute living. He wore long purple robes like a woman, which dragged after him as he went through the market place. He had some planks on his trireme, or warship, cut away, so that his bed did not need to be placed on them but could hang free from beams. His richly gilded shield did not have the usual devices of the Athenians painted on it, but an Eros, or Cupid, holding a thunderbolt in his hand. Decent people at Athens felt disgust and abhorrence at the sight of all this and feared that he might be trying to seize the government, since he held the laws in contempt. Aristophanes, the comic poet, put it well when he said, "They love and hate and cannot do without him."

The truth is that the Athenians endured his excesses because of his generosity, his public shows, the glory of his ancestors, the force of his eloquence, the grace of his person, and his physical strength, with which he combined courage and military knowledge. And so the Athenians indulged him, attributing his faults to youth and good nature. It was he who spoke principally in favor of the attack on the small island of Melos and the slaughter of its inhabitants, simply because they had been neutral in the Peloponnesian War. More than one person said that Greece could not support a second Alcibiades.

Even in the lifetime of Pericles, the Athenians had cast a longing eye on Sicily, but they attempted nothing

until after his death. Then their thoughts turned to attacking the great Sicilian city of Syracuse, which was a
colony of their enemy, Corinth. Alcibiades inflamed this
desire of theirs to a great height and said they should
prepare a vast fleet and conquer the entire island. He gave
the people great hopes, but he entertained even greater
ones for himself. For himself, Sicily was to be merely the
beginning of things, for he dreamed of nothing less than
the conquest of Carthage and Libya. Nicias told the
people that it would be extremely difficult to take Syracuse, but the young men were excited by the thought of
it all, especially by the wonders of the strange countries
they would go to. You could actually see people in public
places drawing on the ground maps of Sicily and Libya
and Carthage.

Socrates opposed the expedition, and so did Meton,
the astronomer. Meton secretly set his house on fire one
night and the next morning begged the Athenians that,
for his comfort and peace of mind after such a calamity,
they should spare his son from the expedition. And this
they did.

After they had voted the expedition, the Athenians
made Nicias general with Alcibiades. They did this
much against Nicias' will, but they thought it wise to
restrain Alcibiades with the caution of Nicias, especially
as Lamachus, the third general, was also impetuous.
When all things had been prepared for the long voyage,
many unlucky omens appeared. One morning the Athe-

nians awoke to find that the stone busts in front of their houses, known as Hermae, had been mutilated during the night. Some people said that Corinthians had done this, to induce Athens to give up its war against Syracuse, their colony. Most people agreed, however, that it had been done by drunken youths.

But as the government looked into the matter further, since the possibility of revolution existed, the charge was made that Alcibiades and some of his friends had once defaced other images in the same way and, moreover, that they had actually profaned the sacred Mysteries of Eleusis. The citizens were outraged, but when they saw that the soldiers and sailors were eager to sail against Sicily, they said that Alcibiades could go and at war's end could answer the charges. Alcibiades demanded an immediate trial, for he perceived the malice in its postponement, but the people ordered him to sail at once.

The armada consisted of 140 triremes, 5,100 heavily armed soldiers, or hoplites, and 1,300 archers and slingers, together with the necessary provisions. But no sooner did they reach Sicily than the Athenians recalled Alcibiades to stand immediate trial. On his way back, Alcibiades gave his captors the slip. The Athenians condemned him for not appearing, confiscated his property, and solemnly cursed him.

Alcibiades took himself to Sparta, where he gave Athens' mortal enemy two pieces of fatal advice. One was to send large forces to reinforce Syracuse and crush

the Athenians there. And the other was to occupy perma-
nently the fort of Decelea, in Attica: this would keep
the people cooped up in Athens all the year and not just
during the summer, as had been the case when the
Peloponnesian War first broke out.

Alcibiades captivated the Spartans by his conformity
to their habits. He wore his hair close-cut, he bathed in
cold water and ate coarse meals, dining on black broth.
People could hardly believe that he ever had a cook in his
house or had been to a perfumer and worn mantles of
Milesian wool. He had the peculiar talent of gaining
men's affections by immediately embracing their ways
of life. He could change color faster than the chameleon.
They say that there is one color the chameleon cannot
assume and that is white, but Alcibiades could adapt
himself with equal ease to the company of good men and
bad and wear the appearance of virtue or vice. At Sparta
he engaged in athletic exercises, was frugal and reserved;
in Ionia in Asia Minor he was luxurious, gay, and in-
dolent; in Thrace he always drank; in Thessaly he was
ever on horseback; and when he lived with Tissaphernes,
the Persian satrap, or governor, he exceeded the Persians
themselves in magnificence and pomp.

After the Athenians had been overwhelmingly defeated in Sicily, Alcibiades helped the Spartans spread a
general revolt in Ionia against Athens. But Agis, the Spartan king, hated him and finally persuaded the magistrates
to send orders to Ionia that Alcibiades was to be killed. As

soon as he heard of this, Alcibiades skipped off to Tissaphernes, the satrap. This Persian was not himself sincere but loved guile and wickedness and admired the subtlety of Alcibiades. Though Tissaphernes was a cruel man and a hater of the Greeks, he was nevertheless so won over by the flatteries of Alcibiades that he tried to exceed them in return. He even named his park in honor of Alcibiades. The park was especially beautiful, with streams and meadows and pavilions and places of retirement royally decorated.

At the suggestion of Alcibiades, Tissaphernes cut down on his aid to the Spartans. This greatly pleased the Athenians, who began to repent of their severe sentence against him. Eventually they recalled Alcibiades, but before he came home, he deserted Tissaphernes and won several important naval victories for Athens in the neighborhood of Asia Minor. Then he set sail for Athens. He adorned the ships of his fleet with shields and other spoils he had taken from the enemy.

As soon as he landed, the crowds pressed in on him and saluted him with loud cheers; they threw flowers at him, and old men proudly pointed him out to the young. Nevertheless, this public joy was mixed with tears, as people remembered that they would not have been defeated in Sicily if they had left Alcibiades in command of their forces. When the assembly had been convened, Alcibiades first lamented his own sufferings and then encouraged the people to continue the war with Sparta. The

Athenians crowned him with crowns of gold and appointed him general, with absolute power by land and sea. They also restored his estates to him and absolved him from the curse they had once solemnly pronounced on him.

There were those at Athens who feared that Alcibiades might be planning to set up a tyranny, and so they were glad when finally he set off with his fleet. At the island of Andros he defeated the Spartans who were there, but could not take the city. This gave his enemies the chance to make further accusations against him. Certainly, if ever a man was ruined by his own glory, it was Alcibiades. His continual successes in the past had produced the idea that if he failed in anything, it was his fault. The Athenians thought that every day they ought to get fresh news of another victory of Alcibiades. They never considered how Alcibiades now lacked money and provisions, while the Persians were constantly supplying the Spartans with all their needs. Lysander, the Spartan admiral, was now operating off the coast of Asia Minor; and once, when Alcibiades had gone in search of supplies, Lysander gained a victory over the Athenian fleet.

Many people in the Athenian fleet hated Alcibiades, and no one more than Thrasybulus. This man now went to Athens and said that Alcibiades was losing ships by neglect of his duties, that he was giving himself over to every kind of luxury and excess and had even fortified a castle in Thrace where, if necessary, he could live out his life instead of in his native Athens. The Athenians responded by choosing other generals. When he heard of this, Alcibiades once again fled for his life.

The new Athenian generals took up their stand at Aegospotami, at the entrance to the Hellespont. They had with them the very last fleet that the Athenians could raise. Every morning they used to sail out to sea and offer battle to Lysander, but when the Spartan refused, they then sailed back again to their base. But they did so without any order, carelessly in contempt of the enemy. Alcibiades, who was nearby, saw their danger and rode down to the generals and pointed out that they lacked a safe harbor, that no town and provisions were in the neighborhood. He also pointed out that the soldiers, when they went ashore, carelessly dispersed and wandered up and down while the enemy's fleet was near them. Finally, he said that the Spartan fleet was disciplined and under the command of a very capable general.

The Athenian generals replied with insults and told him to leave, saying that now they, and not he, commanded the forces. Events, however, soon proved Alcibiades right. Lysander suddenly fell on the Athenians when they least suspected it. Only Conon, an admiral, and eight triremes escaped. The rest of the ships, to the number of 200, Lysander captured, together with 3,000 prisoners, whom he put to death. And then, soon afterward, Lysander captured Athens itself.

Since the Spartans were now masters of Greece by land and sea, Alcibiades stood in dread of them and retired to the Persians in Asia Minor. Lysander, however, realized that as long as Alcibiades lived he was a threat. So he sent a messenger to Pharnabazus, the new Persian satrap, asking him to put Alcibiades to death. Pharnabazus turned the task over to his brother, Magaeus.

At this time Alcibiades was living in a small Phrygian village with Timandra, his mistress. One night he had this dream. He saw himself attired in Timandra's garments; she was holding him in her arms and was painting his face as if he had been a woman. Others say that he dreamed he saw Magaeus cut off his head and burn his body. At any rate, it was only a little while before his death that he had these visions.

Those who had been sent to assassinate Alcibiades did not have the courage to enter his house, but surrounded it and set it on fire. Alcibiades at once threw clothing and furniture on the fire to choke it; and then, wrapping his cloak about his left arm and holding his naked sword in his right hand, rushed out through the middle of the fire. When the Persians saw him, they retreated and, standing at a distance, killed him with their javelins and arrows. Then they departed. Timandra took up Alcibiades' body, wrapped it in her own robes and buried it as decently as her circumstances allowed.

DEMOSTHENES

(384–322 B.C. The fall of Athens and its empire in 404 B.C. meant that first Sparta and then Thebes, under its able general Epaminondas, dominated Greece. The quarreling of the Greek city-states gave a golden opportunity for conquest to the northern kingdom of Macedonia, whose extraordinary king, Philip II, was building a nation of hardy soldiers. Many Greeks—for example, the Athenian orator Aeschines—hoped that Philip might unite the Greeks and stop their warfare. Demosthenes, the greatest of Greek orators and an Athenian patriot, stood for the freedom of Greece. He hurled his stern orations, known as "Philippics," at the Macedonian king. But Philip won in battle against the Greeks at Chaeronea, Plutarch's birthplace, in 338 B.C. Plutarch always insisted that he was writing Lives, not Histories, and in this biography he concentrated on a man's character at a time when deep and complicated issues made it difficult for people to decide on the proper course of action.)

I am not really sure who it was that wrote the poem in honor of Alcibiades, after he had won the chariot race at the Olympic Games, but he tells us that a man to be happy must be born in some famous city. My own opinion is that true happiness is a matter of the mind,

37

and that it is no more of a disadvantage to come from a small city than it is to be born of a small or plain woman. Those arts which have as their end money or honor are likely enough to decay in poor and undistinguished towns; but virtue, like a strong plant, may thrive anywhere it can take hold of a generous nature and an industrious mind. As for my own failings, I shall take the responsibility for them myself and not blame them on my obscure birthplace.

But as for the man who undertakes to write a history that must be compiled from various materials—some of the books being hard to find, and others written in a foreign language—he should indeed live in a large and important city, where there are plenty of books and well-informed people with whom to discuss things. I am willing, however, to continue living in my own small town, so that it will not become any smaller by my departure. When I was in Rome and other parts of Italy, I was so busy with public business and with instructing people in philosophy that I had little time to study the Latin language, and it was only late in life that I learned to read the Latin authors.

And so, in this part of my *Parallel Lives* where I give an account of Demosthenes and Cicero, I shall base my estimate of them simply on their actions and lives as statesmen. The Deity seems to have designed Demosthenes and Cicero on the same plan, giving them many natural similarities—such as their passion for distinction and their love of liberty in civil life, and their lack of courage in dangers and war—and also many accidental resemblances. There can hardly be found two other orators who, from obscure beginnings, became so great and mighty; who both battled with kings and tyrants, lost their daughters, were driven out of their country and returned with honor; who, fleeing once again, were seized by their enemies and finally ended their lives with the liberty of their countrymen. I shall begin with Demosthenes.

Demosthenes' father was an Athenian citizen of good rank, who had a factory that made swords, but it is said of his mother (perhaps slanderously) that she was of lowly birth. This much is certain, that Demosthenes, at the age of seven, was left by his father in comfortable circumstances. His estate amounted to almost fifteen talents [1 talent = $1,800], but his guardians embezzled so much of the money that even his teachers could not be paid. Consequently he did not receive the proper liberal education, and his mother would not let him exert himself on account of his delicate health.

They tell the story that Demosthenes first showed his interest in oratory when a famous orator was about to plead a case, and he heard his teachers say that they were going to the trial. He persuaded them to take him along. When the orator won his case, the young Demosthenes noticed the glory that came to him. From this time on, Demosthenes began to practice oratory. When he became a man, he sued his guardians, and though he was successful, he could recover only a fraction of his inheritance. The experience, however, gave him confidence in public speaking.

But when Demosthenes first addressed the people in their assembly, he was derided for his uncouth style, for his weak voice, and for a shortness of breath that made his sentences disjointed. This so discouraged him that he gave up the assembly for a while. It was at this time that a well-known actor helped him by showing him how to use the proper expression and gestures with his remarks. Now convinced that enunciation and delivery were of the first importance, Demosthenes built himself an underground study, which still stands to this day, and there trained his gestures and voice. Sometimes he would keep at this for two or three months together, shaving one half of his head, so that he would be ashamed to go outside. When he was an old man, Demosthenes used to say that he overcame his defects as follows: his stammering he corrected by speaking with pebbles in his mouth; he disciplined his voice by declaiming speeches when he was out of breath, while running up steep places; and he kept a large mirror in his house, in front of which he practiced his gestures. We will add nothing more to this subject now, but will proceed to an estimate of his character based on his actions and his life as a statesman.

The goal that Demosthenes set for himself in the state was just and noble, namely, the defense of the Greeks against Philip, the Macedonian king. He acted so honorably in this matter that he soon became famous and attracted attention everywhere for his eloquence and courage in speaking. He was admired throughout Greece, the Great King of Persia courted him, and Philip himself esteemed him above all other orators.

In his greatest orations, Demosthenes urges his fellow citizens to pursue not that which seems pleasant or easy or profitable, but to place the just and honorable before their own safety and preservation. If only he had been incorruptible, if his courage in war had only equaled his principles and the dignity of his orations, he would be placed in the highest rank of orators, with men such as Cimon and Pericles. But he lacked courage in battle and was open to bribery, not, to be sure, by Philip, but by Persian gold. Therefore, people said that Demosthenes could recommend the virtues of past times, but could not imitate them. Nevertheless, he far surpassed the other orators of his day, addressed the people boldly, attacked their faults, and opposed their unreasonable desires.

It was evident, even in the period of peace, just what course Demosthenes would steer in Athens. He criticized everything that Philip did and always stirred up the Athenians against him. Consequently, no man was talked about in the Macedonian court as much as Demosthenes. When he went to Macedonia as one of ten ambassadors, his speech was answered with the utmost care and exactness. But in other respects Philip did not enter-tain him as honorably as the rest. And so, when the others congratulated Philip on his eloquence, his handsome physique, and his companionship in drinking, Demosthenes said that the first quality was good enough for a rhetorician, the second for a woman, and the third for a sponge.

When at last war broke out—Philip, on the one side, not being able to live in peace, and the Athenians, on the other, being stirred up by Demosthenes—the first thing Demosthenes did was to persuade the Athenians to capture Euboea, which Philip had won through treachery. Next, Demosthenes sent relief to the people of Byzantium, whom Philip was then attacking. Not long afterward, he went as an envoy throughout Greece, and so inflamed people that he brought most of the city-states together in a league against Philip. The result was that, in addition to the regular troops of citizens, the league raised a mercenary army of 15,000 infantry and 2,000 cavalry. Most people paid in the necessary money cheerfully, but when some states objected, an orator replied, "War can't be fed at so much a day."

Most of the Greek states were in this league, but the hardest task for Demosthenes still lay ahead. This was to get the Thebans to join. Their district, Boeotia, bordered on Attica, of which Athens was the capital; they had large numbers of troops for the war and were regarded as the best soldiers in all Greece. It was no easy thing to persuade them to break with Philip, since on various past

occasions he had helped them; and, besides, Thebes and
Athens often quarreled over frontier questions.

But when Philip, all puffed up with recent successes,
marched south into central Greece, no one knew what to
say, and the Athenian assembly was full of perplexity.
Demosthenes was the only man who advised Athens to
maintain its new alliance with Thebes. This encouraged
the people, raised their spirits and hopes, and accordingly they sent him as ambassador to Thebes. At the
same time Philip sent various envoys there to oppose him.

Now the Thebans knew well enough that it suited
their best interests to remain at peace, and each man had
before his eyes the terrors of war. But such was the force
and power of Demosthenes that he fanned up the
Thebans' courage and so fired them that they cast aside
every thought of prudence, fear, or obligation and, in a
sort of divine passion, chose the path of honor to which
his words invited them. The orator's success was considered so glorious and important that Philip immediately
sent heralds to ask for peace. All Greece promised Thebes
help. Demosthenes now ran the assemblies at both
Thebes and Athens, and everyone held him in high regard.

But, it would seem, there was some divinely ordered
fortune which ordained an end to the liberty of Greece
at this time. Various portents foretold what would
happen, some of them pointing to my little town of
Chaeronea in Boeotia, not far from Thebes. It is not easy

to get at the truth of the matter, but in any case Demosthenes had such confidence in the Greek forces and was
so excited by the sight of many brave men ready to engage the enemy that he would not pay any attention to
portents or oracles. He reminded the Thebans of their
great general of recent days, Epaminondas, and the
Athenians of Pericles. Thus far he behaved like a brave
man. But in the actual battle that followed at Chaeronea
he did nothing honorable, nor did his actions live up to
his speeches. He deserted his place in the battle disgrace-
fully, threw away his arms, and fled.

Philip was so overjoyed by his victory that he actually
went out to view the dead bodies while he was drunk. But
when he came to himself and reflected on his recent
danger, he shuddered at the ability and power of an
orator who had made him risk his life and empire on the
issue of a few brief hours. The fame of the battle even
reached the Persian court, and the Great King sent letters
to his satraps to supply Demosthenes with money, because he was the only Greek able to keep Philip occupied
at home and out of the Persian Empire. Philip's son,
Alexander, later learned about this from certain letters
he found at Sardis in Asia Minor; they told all about
the large sums of money the Persian generals gave to
Demosthenes.

After the defeat at Chaeronea, some of his opponents
at Athens tried to indict Demosthenes, but the people
acquitted him and urged him to continue in public af-

fairs. Thus, when the bones of the Athenians who had been slain at Chaeronea were brought home for solemn burial, he was chosen to deliver the funeral oration. As for Philip, he outlived his victory at Chaeronea by only a couple of years. Demosthenes was the first to get secret news of Philip's death. He seized the occasion to buoy up the people with courage and better hopes for the future and, coming into the assembly with a cheerful countenance, pretended that he had just had a dream that promised good fortune for Athens.

Not much later, messengers arrived with the news of Philip's death. The Athenians at once sacrificed to the gods and voted a crown to Pausanias, the Macedonian who had murdered Philip. Demosthenes appeared in public in a fine robe, with a garland on his head, even though it was only the seventh day since the death of his own daughter. His chief Athenian opponent, the orator Aeschines, criticized him for this, saying that he lacked natural affection for his children. In truth, however, Aeschines betrays a poor spirit and effeminate mind, if he really means that wailings and lamentation are the only signs of a gentle and affectionate nature.

So far as I am concerned, I am unwilling to say that the behavior of the Athenians at this time was wise or honorable. They crowned themselves with garlands and sacrificed to the gods for the death of a king who, when he was victorious and they were conquered, had treated them with clemency and humanity. They had paid him honors while he was alive, and as soon as he had been murdered, they rejoiced and insulted him, as if they had vanquished him by their own valor. At the same time I must commend the behavior of Demosthenes, who left lamentations and sorrows to the women and attended to the business of the city. It should be the duty of any person who is worthy to be in government to stand firm for the public good and maintain the dignity of his character and station. The reason I have let myself say so much about this is because I have known many readers who were melted into unmanly tenderness by the language of Aeschines.

The cities of Greece were inspired once again by Demosthenes to form a league. He sent arms to the Thebans, and they turned on their Macedonian garrison and killed many men. The Athenians made preparations to join forces with the Thebans. Demosthenes was supreme in the popular assembly and wrote letters to the Persian generals to make war upon the Macedonian Alexander, calling him a child and a simpleton. But just as soon as Alexander had settled affairs in his own country and marched with his army into Boeotia, the Athenians lost their courage, and Demosthenes became silent. The Thebans, deserted by Athens, fought by themselves and saw their city destroyed.

The Athenians, in their anxiety, decided to send ambassadors to Alexander and chose Demosthenes as one of them, but he became afraid at the thought of the king's anger and turned back at Mt. Cithaeron. Meanwhile, Alexander sent messengers to Athens and demanded that eight orators be delivered up to him, Demosthenes among them. It was on this occasion that Demosthenes told the Athenians the fable about the sheep who surrender their dogs to the wolves. The dogs in the fable he compared to himself and those like him who protected the people, and Alexander, of course, was the Macedonian wolf. He went on to say, "Just as we see wheat merchants sell their whole stock by a few grains which they carry with them in a dish as a sample, so you Athenians, by delivering us up to Alexander, are surrendering only a few men; but actually, without realizing it, you are surrendering yourselves too." While the Athenians were wondering what to do, one of them volunteered to go to Alexander and intercede with the king on behalf of the orators. Perhaps he relied on his friendship with Alexander, or perhaps he hoped to find Alexander satiated, as a lion glutted with slaughter. At any rate, he prevailed on Alexander to pardon the men and to be reconciled to Athens.

So, after Alexander had gone home, Demosthenes had little influence at Athens. Then, when Alexander left for Asia, Demosthenes welcomed the revolt of the Spartan Agis, but only briefly, for the Athenians would not support him. Agis was killed in battle, and the Spartans were defeated.

It was about this time that Ctesiphon was brought to

trial at Athens. A few years earlier—around the time of
the battle at Chaeronea—Ctesiphon had proposed that a
crown be given Demosthenes for his public services;
Aeschines had then indicted Ctesiphon for making an
illegal proposal. The case now came to trial, and Demosthenes made one of his most famous speeches, called "On
the Crown," in defense of Ctesiphon. This became the
most celebrated case at Athens, not only because of the
fame of the orators, but also because of the courage of
the judges. After all, the accusers of Demosthenes—
Aeschines and the pro-Macedonian faction—were at the
height of their power and were supported by the Macedonian government. Nevertheless, the judges acquitted
Demosthenes honorably, and Aeschines then withdrew
to the island of Rhodes and to Ionia, in Asia Minor,
where he spent the rest of his life teaching rhetoric.

Not much later Harpalus, Alexander's treasurer, fled
from Asia to Athens. His love of luxury had led him to
embezzle large sums of money, and he now feared the
king, who was harsh even with his friends. Well, Harpalus put himself, his wealth, and his ships at the disposal of the Athenians. All the other orators, having their
eyes fixed on so much money, came to Harpalus' aid
and urged the people to receive the suppliant. Demosthenes, however, at first advised them to drive Harpalus
from the city, lest they become involved in an unneces-
sary war. It then happened, a few days later when they
were counting the treasures, that Harpalus noticed

Demosthenes looking with much pleasure at a Persian cup and its ornamentation. So he told Demosthenes to hold the cup in his hand and feel the weight of the gold. Demosthenes was amazed how heavy the gold was and asked what its weight *came to.* "To you," Harpalus replied, smiling, "it will *come with* twenty talents." That night he sent the cup with twenty talents to Demosthenes. Harpalus had the extraordinary ability to discover a man's covetousness by his expression and the movement of his eyes.

Demosthenes could not resist the temptation, but accepted the present and thus surrendered himself to the interests of Harpalus. The very next day he came to the meeting of the assembly with his neck all wrapped up in woolen bandages, and when he was called on to rise and speak, he made signs as if he had lost his voice. The wits of the town, however, ridiculed him and said that he had been seized during the night, not with a regular quinsy, but with a silver quinsy. When the people learned about the bribery, they were angry with Demosthenes and would not let him speak or apologize, but shouted him down. They then banished Harpalus from Athens.

Demosthenes was fined fifty talents for his part in the affair and was put in prison. With the help of some friends, he made his escape, but he did not show much fortitude in his exile. He spent his time on the island of Aegina and on the opposite Peloponnesian coast, in Troezen, with tears in his eyes as he looked across at Attica.

Some of his sayings are on record, and these hardly re-
semble the sentiments of generosity and bravery which he
expressed when he was in charge of the government. For
example, as he was leaving Athens, he raised his hands
toward the Acropolis and said, "O goddess Athena, how
can you delight in three such beasts, the owl, the snake,
and the people?"

Alexander died while Demosthenes was still in exile.
Immediately many Greeks rose up in arms against Antipater, Alexander's regent in Macedonia. Demosthenes
urged the cities to drive the Macedonians out of Greece.
This conduct now pleased the Athenians, and they sent
a ship to Aegina and brought him back to Piraeus,
Athens' harbor. All the citizens met him with joy. We
are told that Demosthenes, on landing, lifted up his
hands toward heaven and blessed this day of his happy
return. He said his return from exile was more honorable
than Alcibiades', for his countrymen had recalled him by
their own free will and not by threat of force. The people
then remitted his fine of fifty talents. But he enjoyed his
country for only a short time, because the Greeks were
soon defeated by the Macedonians, and a Macedonian
garrison was placed in Piraeus.

Not much later Demosthenes died in the following
manner. When he heard that Antipater was approaching
Athens, he escaped secretly from the city. The people
then condemned him to death, and Antipater sent some
soldiers, under Archias, to find him. Archias learned that

Demosthenes had fled for sanctuary to the temple of Poseidon on the island of Calauria. So he sailed over to the island with his troops and tried to persuade Demosthenes to accompany him to Antipater, as if he would suffer nothing from the Macedonian. However, Demosthenes had had a strange dream the night before, to the effect that he was contending with Archias for a prize in a tragedy and had won the favor of the spectators, but had lost because of his stage arrangements.

So now, while Archias was talking with him in friendly fashion, Demosthenes just sat there and stared at him. Finally he said, "Archias, I am no more impressed by your promises today than I formerly was by your acting." This made Archias angry, and he began to threaten him. Demosthenes then said, "You were acting a part before, Archias, but now you speak like a true Macedonian. Please, therefore, wait a few moments, while I write a letter to my family."

With these words, Demosthenes went back into the temple and took out a scroll, as if he meant to write. He put the reed pen into his mouth and bit it, as he always did when he was thinking or writing, and held it there some time. Then he bowed down his head and covered it. The soldiers at the door, thinking that he lacked courage, called him a coward, and Archias came in and told him to get up and promised him again a reconciliation with Antipater. Demosthenes now realized that the poison had taken hold of him. He uncovered his head and, fixing his eyes on Archias, said, "You may throw my body out unburied. But, beloved Poseidon, while I am still alive, I will leave this sacred place, though Antipater and the Macedonians would not have left even your temple unpolluted." He then rose and, asking someone to help him because he was already trembling, he left the temple, and just as he passed the altar, he fell down and died. He died on a specially solemn day of the month, and not long afterward the people of Athens voted him the honors he deserved and ordered a bronze statue to be made of him.

The following incident occurred just a little while before I myself went to Athens, four centuries after Demosthenes' death. A soldier was ordered to appear before his officer and answer to a certain accusation. When he saw this statue of Demosthenes, he put a small piece of gold in one of the hands; the fingers of the hand were bent. Nearby stood a plane tree, and many leaves were either blown by the wind on to the statue or were placed there deliberately by the soldier to hide his money. At any rate, he eventually came back and found the gold intact. The story spread through Athens. Many people said that the incident proved the integrity of Demosthenes and wrote epigrams on the subject.

Various Athenian opponents of Demosthenes were ultimately executed by the Macedonians. They thus learned, as Demosthenes himself used to declare, that traitors who sell their country sell themselves first.

And so, Sosius—my Roman friend to whom I dedi-
cate this biography—you have the life of Demosthenes,
based on what I have been able to read and hear about
him.

ALEXANDER THE GREAT

(356–323 B.C. The chief fault of the Greek city-states was their failure to form a wider union, and thus they fell an easy prey to Macedonia, a rough mountain kingdom on the northern edge of Greece. In 338 B.C. at Chaeronea, in central Greece, Philip II of Macedon and his son, Alexander, defeated the Greeks and joined them in the so-called League of Corinth in a war to punish the hereditary enemy, Persia, for its invasion of Greece in the previous century. Two years later, Philip was murdered, and Alexander, now twenty years old, carried through the plan. He is famous as the conqueror of the civilized world, but he also dreamed of brotherhood among peoples. During the three centuries after his death —that is, until the Roman conquest—most of the world that he conquered adopted a common Greek culture; it was ruled, moreover, by his Macedonian successors.)

Alexander was descended on his father's side from Heracles and on his mother's from Aeacus, both of them famous Greek heroes. When his father, Philip, was young and was visiting on the Aegean island of Samothrace, he fell in love with a fiery princess from Epirus, Olympias by name. Not much later, Philip and Olympias were initiated into some religious ceremonies of the country, and then they were married.

Alexander was born the following summer on the very same day, so people said later, that the temple of Artemis at Ephesus, in Asia Minor, burned to the ground in honor of the event. And so three messages were brought at the same time to Philip, who had just captured Potidaea: that his general, Parmenio, had defeated the Illyrians in battle, that his horse had won a race at the Olympic Games, and that his wife had given birth to Alexander. The seers added to Philip's delight by saying that a son, whose birth coincided with such victories, would be invincible.

Alexander was fair in color, medium in height, and had the habit of bending his head toward the left shoulder. Even as a boy he was moderate in his pleasures and did not always seek glory, as his father did. When someone asked him if he would compete at the Olympic Games, since he was a fast runner, he replied that he would if he might have kings to run against. He was not very fond of athletics, though he did enjoy giving prizes to tragedians and musicians, and he loved to hunt.

Whenever Alexander heard that Philip had captured some important place, instead of rejoicing completely, he would say to his companions that nothing would be left for them to do. For he was more interested in action and glory than in pleasures and riches.

Once a Thessalian brought a horse, Bucephalus by

name, to Philip and offered to sell it for thirteen talents
[1 talent = $1,800]. But when they brought the horse
out to the field, to try it, they found it unmanageable and
were about to lead it away. Alexander called out, "What
a wonderful horse they are losing because they can't manage it." At first, Philip pretended not to hear, but when
Alexander repeated it, Philip said, "Can you manage the
horse better than people who are older than you?" Alexander said that he certainly could manage this horse better and bet its price.

Everyone began to laugh. But Alexander ran to the
horse and, taking hold of the bridle, turned it toward the
sun, for he had noticed that the horse was frightened by
its shadow. Then he mounted the horse and, little by
little, let it go at full speed. Philip and the others at first
looked on in silence, very much worried, but when they
saw Alexander turn at the end of the course and come
back in triumph, they all cheered, and Philip actually
shed tears of joy and said to Alexander, as he dismounted,
"My son, seek out a kingdom worthy of yourself, for
Macedonia is too small for you."

Philip then engaged Aristotle, the most famous philosopher of the day, as teacher for Alexander. Alexander
learned much about morals and politics from Aristotle,
and also about medicine. In fact, he learned from Aristotle to be curious about all sorts of things, and when he
set off on his famous expedition to Asia, he brought along

a copy of Homer's *Iliad* which Aristotle had edited, and kept it with his dagger under his pillow at night.

Alexander was only twenty years old when a Macedonian noble murdered Philip. Thus he succeeded to a kingdom that was surrounded by enemies, not only by barbarians to the north, but also by the Greeks southward, whom Philip had only recently conquered. With lightning speed, Alexander marched north to the River Danube, conquering as he went, and then returned to Greece. First he destroyed Thebes, a great city that had revolted from him, and then he summoned representatives of all the Greeks to meet him at Corinth. Here he was proclaimed commander in chief in a war against the Persian Empire, which more than a century earlier had invaded Greece.

While Alexander was at Corinth, many statesmen and philosophers came from all parts of Greece to congratulate him. But, contrary to his expectation, Diogenes of Sinope, who was actually living in a suburb of Corinth at the time, did not so much as stir. So Alexander went to the philosopher and found him lying in the sun. When Diogenes saw Alexander and his friends near him, he raised himself up a little and looked at Alexander. Alexander asked him if he wanted anything, and Diogenes replied, "Yes, stand out of the sun." Alexander was so struck by the answer and by the greatness of the man, who took such little notice of him, that as they were going away he said to his friends, who were laughing, that if he were not Alexander he would choose to be Diogenes.

Alexander was twenty-two years old when he crossed the Hellespont [the Dardanelles] from Europe to Asia with an army of 30,000 infantry and 5,000 cavalry. First he went to Troy where he sacrificed to the goddess Athena and anointed the grave of Achilles, the great Greek hero of the Trojan War. He said that Achilles was fortunate in having so famous a poet as Homer to relate his deeds.

Alexander next went to the River Granicus, where he found the enemy waiting for him: they were drawn up in battle formation under the generals of Darius, the Great King of the mighty Persian Empire. Alexander charged the enemy almost at once, leading his cavalry on the right wing down into the river and up the steep bank opposite. All this time the Persians were hurling missiles at the Macedonians, and some charged Alexander himself, for he could be easily recognized by the large plume of white feathers on each side of his helmet. Two Persian commanders fell on Alexander together. While Alexander was killing one, the other Persian rose up in his saddle and landed such a blow with his battle axe on Alexander's head that it broke the helmet. He was just about to hit Alexander another blow when Alexander's friend Cleitus—Black Cleitus as he was called—ran his spear through the Persian.

All this time that the cavalry were fighting, the Macedonian infantry, formed in their phalanx, were also vigorously crossing the river. Alexander won a tremendous victory, losing only a few of his own men, while several thousand of the Persians were killed. He sent 300 shields to the Athenians as a memento of the battle, and some Persian drinking cups and purple garments to his mother.

Sardis, which was the provincial capital of the Persians, now surrendered to Alexander, as did all the Greek cities along the coast of Asia Minor, except for Miletus and Halicarnassus; these he had to storm on account of their Persian garrisons. Alexander then turned inland to Gordium in Phrygia. Here he saw the famous chariot fastened with cords made of the bark of the cornel tree. According to tradition, the man who untied the Gordian knot would be master of the world. Most of the ancient authors say that when Alexander found he couldn't untie the knot (because its ends were hidden), he cut it with his sword.

By this time, King Darius was marching from his administrative capital at Susa, full of confidence in his 600,-000 soldiers. His confidence increased still more when Alexander delayed at Tarsus in Cilicia, for he attributed this to cowardice. Actually, however, Alexander was sick. When his condition became critical, Philip of Acarnania —his friend and physician—brought him medicine to drink. It so happened that Alexander had just received a letter from Parmenio, his general, telling him to watch out for this Philip, because he had been bribed by Darius to kill him and had been promised a daughter in marriage.

It was a spectacle really worthy of the theater, because when Philip came in with the medicine, Alexander gave him the letter; and, while Philip read it, Alexander took the drink. They then turned and looked at one another, but with different sentiments—Alexander's looks were happy and full of confidence in his friend, while Philip deeply resented the accusation. It was not long before the medicine made Alexander completely well.

The two armies met at Issus in Cilicia. Fortunately for Alexander, this was a narrow plain where Darius' superior numbers could not be used. Alexander won another tremendous victory, though he was wounded in the thigh. Darius, however, fled, but Alexander was unable to catch him. When he returned from the pursuit, Alexander found that his friends had set aside for him the tent of Darius, which was full of gold and silver and splendid furniture. After he had taken off his armor, Alexander went to the bath, saying, "Let us now wash in the bath of Darius." "Not at all," replied one of his friends, "but in Alexander's, because the property of the conquered belongs to the conqueror." And when Alexander saw all the gold and ointment boxes, and smelled the fragrant odors, and then passed into a large pavilion, where couches and tables had been prepared for a magnificent entertainment by Darius, he turned to his friends and said, "This, apparently, is what it means to be a king."

As he was going off to supper, a message was brought

Alexander that among the Persian prisoners were Darius' mother and wife and two unmarried daughters, and that they were mourning for Darius. Alexander sent them word that Darius was not dead and that they need have no fear for themselves, because they would be provided with everything they had been accustomed to receive from Darius. This was typical of Alexander, for he thought it more kingly to govern himself than to conquer his enemies.

Alexander was far less addicted to wine than was generally believed. The false belief arose from the fact that, when he had nothing else to do, he loved to sit long and talk, as he slowly drank. But when business called him, he would not be detained, as other generals often were, either by wine or sleep or love affairs, by spectacles or any other diversion. A proof of this is that, in the short time he lived, he accomplished so much that was great.

On a free day Alexander, after rising and sacrificing to the gods, used to have breakfast and then spend the rest of the day hunting or writing or reading or deciding a military question. On the march, if no special speed was required, he would practice shooting as he went along, or mount a chariot and alight from it at full speed. Sometimes, too, as the Royal Journal tells us, he would hunt foxes and birds.

In the evening, after he had bathed and anointed himself, he would call for his bakers and chief cooks and ask whether dinner was ready. He never cared to dine till it was pretty late and beginning to get dark, and he was wonderfully careful that all his guests should be served alike and with proper attention. He would, at the end, love to sit long with his wine and talk, as has been said. And then, though in other respects no other prince's conversation was ever more agreeable, he would fall into soldierly boasting, which gave his flatterers an opening and made his friends uneasy.

Instead of pursuing Darius after Issus, Alexander thought it first necessary to get to the seacoast of the eastern Mediterranean. In this way he would capture the bases of the enemy's fleet and force it to come over to his side. The island of Cyprus surrendered to him, and so did the cities of Phoenicia, excepting only Tyre. He besieged this city for seven months with mounds of earth and battering rams, and two hundred triremes by sea. He was encouraged to persist because of a dream in which he saw Heracles on the walls, reaching out his hands and calling to him.

During the siege of Tyre, Alexander made an excursion against the Arabs in the Antilebanon Mountains, in which he risked his life to save an old tutor, Lysimachus by name, who insisted on going with him. After they had left their horses and had begun to go up the hills on foot, most of the soldiers got far ahead, but Alexander stayed with Lysimachus, because it was almost night and the enemy were near. Before he was fully aware of it, Alexander was left behind with only a few soldiers and was forced to spend an extremely cold night in the dark and in a very inconvenient place. Then, suddenly, he saw a great many fires of the enemy, scattered about at a distance, and since he trusted in his own agility and was always ready to undergo toils to cheer any Macedonians in distress, he ran straight to one of the nearest fires. He killed two of the enemy with his dagger, snatched up a lighted brand and brought it back to his own men. They immediately made a large fire which so alarmed the enemy that most of them fled, and those that assaulted them were soon routed. Thus they spent the rest of the night in safety.

Alexander ultimately destroyed Tyre and then marched to Egypt. It seemed to him that the island of Pharos, just above the Canobic mouth of the River Nile, was an excellent situation for a city, with lagoons on one side and the sea on the other, thus making possible a spacious harbor. He told his men to start laying out the city [named Alexandria, after him], while he himself went to visit the temple of Ammon, an oracle in an oasis of the desert to the west.

This was a long and dangerous journey. For one thing, they might run out of water. For another, a violent south wind might blow while they were traveling through the deep sands—as actually happened once to the Persian king Cambyses and his army, when great masses of sand buried 50,000 of his men. In this journey, Alexander was aided by the gods. Plentiful rains fell. And then,

when the guides lost the way and there were no land-
marks to direct them, they were set right by some ravens
that flew ahead of them on the march.

When they had passed through the desert to the oasis
and had reached the temple, the priest welcomed Alexander in the name of Alexander's father, Ammon. Then
Alexander asked if any of his father's murderers had escaped punishment, but the priest told him to speak more
respectfully, since his was not a mortal father. So Alexander changed his expression and asked if any of Philip's
murderers had escaped, and then whether the empire of
the world was to be his. The priest said he would obtain
this and that Philip's death was fully avenged. Alexander
was so pleased that he made splendid offerings to the god
and gave the priest rich presents.

That is the account most authors give about the oracle.
But in a letter to his mother, Alexander tells her that
there were some secret answers, which on his return he
would tell to her and her only.

Alexander met a philosopher named Psammon in
Egypt. The saying of Psammon which he liked best
was to the effect that all men are governed by God, because in everything that which is chief and commands
is divine. But Alexander was even more philosophical
when he added that God was the common father of us
all, and especially of the best of us.

To the barbarians [i.e., to the foreigners] Alexander
carried himself haughtily, as if mindful of divine birth,

but to the Greeks he affected little. In fact, on one occasion when he had been wounded by an arrow, he said, "This, my friends, is real blood flowing here and not, in Homer's words, Ichor, such as immortal gods shed." And another time, when a clap of thunder frightened everyone, Anaxarchus, the sophist, asked him if he, who was Zeus' son, could do that. "No," said Alexander, laughing, "I have no desire to be formidable to my friends." And so it is clear that Alexander merely used his claims of divinity as a way to maintain the sense of his superiority among others.

On Alexander's return to Phoenicia, Darius wrote him a letter, asking him to accept as a ransom for his royal captives the sum of 10,000 talents, a daughter in marriage, and all the lands this side of the River Euphrates. When Alexander communicated this to his friends, Parmenio said, "If I were Alexander, I would accept." "So would I," Alexander replied, "if I were Parmenio." Accordingly, he told Darius that he would be treated with kindness if he came and surrendered; otherwise, he would at once go himself and seek him.

The great battle between Darius and Alexander was fought east of the River Tigris at Gaugamela and not, as most authors state, at Arbela, a town several miles away. The night before the battle Darius kept his men under arms and reviewed them by torchlight. Alexander, on the other hand, told his soldiers to sleep. He himself spent the night in front of his tent with his seer, Aristander, performing certain mysterious ceremonies and sacrificing to the god Fear.

Meanwhile, when Parmenio and the other generals saw the plain all lighted up by the campfires of the enemy, whose voices sounded like the roar of a vast ocean, they decided it would be difficult to fight such an immense army in the daylight. Accordingly, after Alexander had finished sacrificing, they urged him to attack Darius under cover of darkness. But Alexander gave them the celebrated reply, "I will not steal my victory."

Alexander then lay down in his tent and slept, the rest of the night, more soundly than usual. This astonished his officers the next morning, and they themselves had to order the soldiers to take breakfast. At last, Parmenio went to Alexander's bedside and called him a couple of times by name. When he was awake, he asked him how, when he was about to fight his most important battle, he could sleep soundly as if he were already victorious. Alexander smiled and said, "We are indeed already victorious, for at last we don't have to pursue Darius through a wide countryside."

On the morning of the battle, Alexander came out of his tent and put on his helmet. He was wearing a Sicilian coat with a breastplate over it. His sword was of fine, light steel. As long as he was drawing up his men, he spared Bucephalus, who was now growing old, and used another horse. But when he was ready to attack, he sent for Bucephalus and mounted him.

First Alexander addressed the Greeks and Macedonians in stirring fashion. Then the seer Aristander, who wore a white mantle and a golden crown on his head, rode by and pointed out an eagle that soared just over Alexander and directed its flight toward the enemy. This wonderfully encouraged the beholders.

The Macedonian cavalry now charged at full speed, followed by the phalanx of infantry. Before they could come to blows, the front ranks of the enemy retreated. Alexander hotly pursued them and drove them into the middle of the Persian line, where Darius was. He could see Darius, who was conspicuous in the midst of his guards, a tall and fine-looking man, drawn in a high chariot and defended by his best cavalry. Alexander's onslaught was now so terrible that those who stood their ground were slain.

Darius soon realized that all was lost, but the wheels of his chariot got caught in the dead bodies lying around, and the driver could hardly manage the frightened horses. So he left his arms and chariot and mounted a horse and fled. He would not have escaped, if Parmenio had not sent word to Alexander that the Bactrian cavalry were pressing him hard. Regretfully, Alexander abandoned the pursuit of Darius, but on the way back learned that Parmenio had finally prevailed.

The battle seemed to put an end to the Persian Empire. Alexander was proclaimed King of Asia and rendered thanks to the gods in magnificent sacrifices and rewarded his friends and followers with rich presents. Thence he marched through Babylonia, which immediately surrendered to him.

Here Alexander and his men were much surprised at the sight of a place where fire kept spouting; nearby, a stream of naphtha was flowing out of the ground. This naphtha will light, even if it is only near a flame. The Babylonians sprinkled the street leading to Alexander's quarters with little drops of the naphtha and then, when it was almost night, they lit the drops at the far end of the street. Instantly the whole street caught fire.

When he took Susa, Alexander found in the palace 40,000 talents of coined money, and much furniture and other treasure. For example, there were 5,000 talents' weight of Phoenician purple, which had been stored there for 190 years. One ancient author says that the Persian kings also stored up water from the Nile and Danube to suggest the greatness of their universal empire.

Alexander had to fight to enter Persia proper, but eventually he won through to Persepolis, the capital. Great treasure was taken here, too. He rested his soldiers in Persepolis for four months.

One evening Alexander gave a magnificent entertainment for his officers. In the course of it, an Athenian woman named Thais—she was the mistress of Alexander's general Ptolemy, who later became King of Egypt —said she would love to set fire to the palace of Xerxes, who had burned Athens in his invasion of Greece the previous century. She said it would be fine for posterity to record that the women who followed Alexander had taken vengeance on the Persians. Everyone applauded, and then they all went around with torches and burned the palace down. Some ancient writers, however, say that Alexander burned the palace to show the world that one regime, the Persian, had ended; and everyone agrees that Alexander soon repented and ordered the fire to be put out.

Alexander was naturally most generous and grew more so as his riches increased. Olympias wrote him that he should be more moderate in his rewards. "For now," she said, "you make all these people equal to kings." His mother often wrote him in this way, but he never communicated her letters to anyone, except to his close friend, Hephaestion. He never let her meddle in public affairs, however. Once, when he read a long letter full of accusations against her from Antipater, his regent in Macedonia, Alexander said, "Antipater does not know that one tear of a mother effaces a thousand letters such as this."

Alexander now set out to find Darius, expecting another battle, but he soon learned that Darius had been seized by the Bactrian prince, Bessus. The pursuit of Darius proved long and difficult, for in the course of eleven days Alexander rode over 400 miles. This exhausted his soldiers, and many were ready to give up, chiefly for lack of water. It so happened one noon that some Macedon-

ians were bringing water from a stream in skins, and seeing Alexander almost choked with thirst, filled a helmet
and offered it to him. Alexander asked them for whom
they were carrying the water and they said, for their children; but, they added, if his life was saved, their children did not matter. Alexander refused to take a drop.
"For," he said, "if I drink, the rest will be discouraged."
When the soldiers heard this, they cried out to him to
lead them forward and began to whip their horses. While
they had such a king, they said, they could defy both
weariness and thirst.

Although they were all equally cheerful and willing,
only about 60 of them could keep up with Alexander and
fall upon the enemy's camp. Here they rode over quantities of gold and silver that lay scattered about and passed
many chariots full of women, but without drivers. They
pressed on, hoping to see Darius, and at last they found
him, lying in a chariot, wounded all over with javelins.
He sent Alexander a few words of thanks for his kindness
to his family and then died. When Alexander came up,
he was sad and covered the body with his own cloak.

Alexander then marched past the Caspian Sea into
Parthia. It was here that he put on Persian dress for the
first time, thinking, perhaps, that this would make the
task of civilizing the natives easier, for nothing appeals
to men quite so much as conforming to their customs.
At first he wore this dress only when he talked with foreigners, or indoors among his intimate friends, but af-

terward he appeared in it when he rode out, and at public audiences. This offended the Macedonians, but they so respected his good qualities that they thought it reasonable to gratify his passion for glory.

And so Alexander more and more adjusted his way of living to that of the natives and tried to bring them as close as possible to Macedonian customs. He thought it wise to depend on the good will which would come from a mixture of customs, rather than on force. To further this idea, he chose 30,000 native boys and put them under instructors to teach them the Greek language and to train them in the use of Macedonian weapons.

And while he was in Bactria [northern Afghanistan], Alexander married the beautiful young princess, Roxane. It was a love affair, and yet it seemed to contribute to the plans he had in mind, for it pleased the conquered people to see him choose a wife from among themselves.

It was about this time that Alexander's friend Philotas, the son of Parmenio, conspired against him and was put to death, as was also Parmenio. Not long afterward came the unhappy affair of Cleitus, the same Black Cleitus who had saved Alexander's life at the Granicus. Both Cleitus and Alexander had drunk far too much at a banquet, they taunted one another, and finally some friends pushed Cleitus out of the room. But he came back again by another door, singing a verse from Euripides, "In Greece, alas! what an evil government!" Alexander thereupon snatched a spear from a guard and ran Cleitus through. His anger left him immediately, and he pulled the spear out of the dead body and would have thrust it into his own throat, if the guards had not held his hands and carried him into his chamber. Here all that night and the next day he wept bitterly.

Alexander next marched into India. At the Indus River he met King Taxiles, with whom he exchanged gifts of friendship, and then continued eastward toward the kingdom of Porus. In his own letters Alexander has given an account of his battle with Porus. He says that the two armies were separated by the River Hydaspes; on the opposite bank Porus continually kept the elephants in battle order, with their heads pointing toward the enemy, to guard the crossing. Alexander himself, however, made a loud noise every day in his camp, to accustom the enemy to it and thus decrease their fears. Then one dark stormy night he crossed the river, at some distance from the camp of the enemy, to a little island, with some of his infantry and his best cavalry. It now began to rain violently, with lightning and high winds, but nevertheless he left the island and crossed to the other side. The Hydaspes was so swollen by the rain that the men had to wade across the ford up to their breasts in water.

Once across, Alexander was attacked by a contingent of the enemy made up of 1,000 cavalry and 60 armed chariots, but he destroyed most of them then and there. Porus now guessed that Alexander himself had crossed;

so, leaving a small party in camp to oppose the Macedonians opposite, he marched with his whole army against Alexander. Because of the large size of the enemy's army, and to avoid the shock of the elephants, Alexander divided his forces. He attacked Porus' left wing himself and ordered his general, Coenus, to fall upon the right. Thus both wings of the enemy were broken; they then fell back in their retreat on the center and crowded in upon the elephants. A hand-to-hand battle raged till the eighth hour of the day before the Indians were utterly defeated.

Almost all the ancient historians agree that Porus was six feet three inches tall, and that when he was on his huge elephant, his size made it appear that he was fittingly mounted. This elephant, during the whole battle, defended its king with great courage, driving off those who attacked. But when the elephant saw that Porus had been wounded and might fall off, it softly knelt down and began to draw out the missiles with its proboscis. When Porus was taken prisoner, and Alexander asked him how he expected to be treated, he answered, "Like a king." And when the same question was put to him a second time, he said that that expression summed up everything. Alexander, accordingly, allowed Porus to govern his own kingdom as satrap under himself.

Not long after the battle with Porus, Alexander's horse Bucephalus died, either because of wounds or old age. Alexander was deeply affected by this, and built a city on the bank of the Hydaspes, which he named Bucephala in his memory.

But this battle with Porus took the edge off the Macedonians' courage, and soon they refused to march farther east. The rumor of multitudes of enemies and thousands of elephants was too much for them. Alexander at first was so angry with his men that he shut himself up in his tent and declared that to retreat now was to confess defeat. At last, however, the reasonable advice of his friends and the suppliant cries of his soldiers induced him to think of turning back.

Alexander was now eager to see the Indian Ocean. He caused many boats and rafts to be built. On the way down the Hydaspes and Indus rivers, he took various fortified towns. But during the siege of the town of the Mallians, who reputedly were the bravest people of India, he almost lost his life. He was the first man to mount their wall by a scaling ladder. But as soon as he was up, the ladder broke, leaving him almost alone and exposed to the enemy's missiles. Alexander then jumped down into their midst. When the Indians saw that only two companions accompanied Alexander, they charged; and one Indian shot an arrow at Alexander which went right through his breastplate and stuck in his ribs under the chest. This blow was so violent that Alexander staggered back and placed a knee on the ground. In this manner he killed several Indians, but they kept charging him until at last he received such a blow on his head from a club that he had to lean his body against the wall. At this point the Macedonians broke down the wall and forced their way in. They picked Alexander up, just as he was fainting away, and carried him to his tent. It was soon reported all through the camp that he was dead.

With great difficulty the Macedonians sawed off the wooden shaft of the arrow and then removed Alexander's breastplate. However, the head of the arrow was three fingers broad and four long and was stuck fast in the bone. During the operation Alexander swooned and almost died, but when the arrow was out, he slowly came to. For a long time he was weak and rested himself, until one day the Macedonians began shouting and insisted on seeing him. Accordingly, he put on his cloak and went out. After the rejoicing for his recovery, he sacrificed to the gods.

In his voyage down the rivers to the ocean, Alexander captured ten Indian philosophers, known as Gymnosophists, who were supposed to be very clever at answering questions. So Alexander decided to ask them difficult questions, and said that those who answered incorrectly would be put to death. He made the oldest Gymnosophist judge.

The first one, being asked which were the more numerous, the dead or the living, said the living were, since the dead did not exist. The second was asked whether the earth or the sea produced larger beasts; he replied that the earth did, for the sea is but a part of it. The third was asked which animal was the most cunning, and he replied, "That which man has not yet discovered." The fourth was asked why he had persuaded a local ruler to revolt. "Because," he answered, "I wanted him either to live or die nobly." The fifth, being asked which was older, day or night, said, "Day, by one day." Alexander expressed his astonishment, and the Indian explained that hard questions had to have hard answers. Then Alexander asked the next what a man had to do to be really loved. "He must be very powerful," the Indian replied, "without being feared." The seventh, being asked how a man might become a god, answered, "By doing that which a man cannot do." Alexander asked the next Indian which was stronger, life or death, and he replied, "Life, because it supports so many miseries." And the last, when he was asked how long it was right for a man to live, said, "Until death appears more desirable than life."

Alexander then turned to the judge and ordered him to give his sentence. The Indian said that in his opinion each had answered worse than another. Alexander finally dismissed them with presents. On another occasion, however, an Indian philosopher named Calanus decided to accompany Alexander on his expedition.

The voyage down the rivers took seven months. When Alexander finally reached the ocean, he sacrificed to the gods. He made Nearchus admiral of his fleet and ordered him to sail to Mesopotamia, with the Indian shore on his right hand. Alexander himself marched with his army through a vast desert, with little water or food, and many of his men died. Finally, however, he reached Carmania, where provisions had been gathered for him.

Here Nearchus joined him, and Alexander was so thrilled with his narrative of the voyage that he decided to sail from the mouth of the Euphrates around Arabia and Africa and enter the Mediterranean by way of the Pillars of Heracles. Therefore he ordered ships to be built and crews collected.

In Persia, Alexander found that someone had rifled the tomb of Cyrus. He was deeply moved by the inscription on the tomb, for it reminded him of the uncertainty and mutability of human affairs: "O man, whoever you are, and wherever you come from (for I know you will come), I am Cyrus, the founder of the Persian Empire. Do not begrudge me this little earth which covers my body."

At the same time Calanus, the Indian philosopher who had joined Alexander, announced that he wished to have a funeral pyre erected for him. When this had been done, he came on horseback, said a few prayers, sprinkled himself, and threw some of his hair on the pyre. He told the Macedonians to have a day of feasting with Alexander, whom he expected to see soon again at Babylon. Then he climbed the pyre, lay down on it, and did not stir as the flames came close to him. Thus he sacrificed himself, as philosophers of his country often did.

At Susa, Alexander married Stateira, Darius' daughter, and celebrated the weddings of his companions who married noble Persian women. He paid the debts of his soldiers. Not long afterward, however, his close friend, Hephaestion, died, one of Alexander's saddest blows.

When Alexander came to Babylon, all kinds of unfavorable omens were reported. And then, as it happened, he was seized with a fever. The Royal Journal gives a minute account of Alexander's last days. It tells how Alexander talked with his officers, and especially with Nearchus, about the exploring expedition around Arabia. It also tells how he sacrificed each day as long as he had the strength. Finally he became speechless, and his Macedonians, thinking him dead, forced their way in and passed by his bedside. That same day, toward evening, he died.

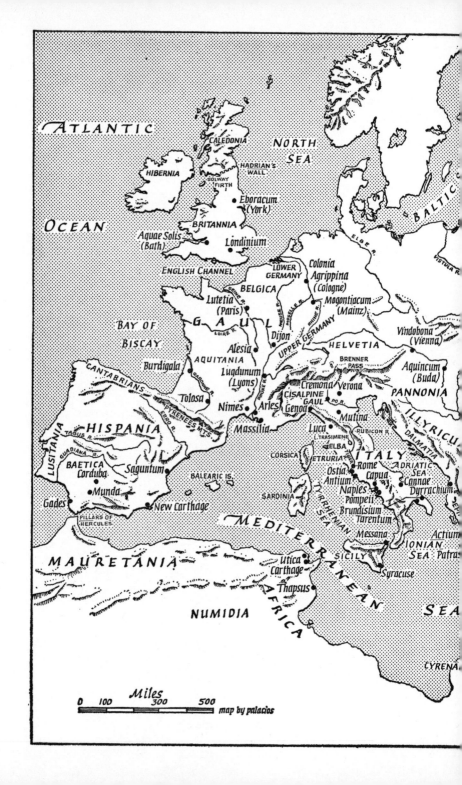

The
ROMAN EMPIRE

FABIUS

*(Died 203 B.C. The Second Punic War, 218–201
B.C., was perhaps the most terrible conflict in antiquity.
Carthage, the ancient state in Africa, possessed in Hannibal one of the world's great military geniuses. His
first victories in Italy caused the Romans to appoint as
dictator Quintus Fabius Maximus. The scheme of Fabius
was not to meet Hannibal in open battle, where defeat
was probable, but to wear him down by dogging his
tracks, a policy that won him the title of* Cunctator, *"the
Delayer." Rome's ultimate victory over Hannibal meant,
in effect, that she was surely destined to conquer and
rule the civilized world.)*

According to the story, the founder of the famous
family of Fabius was born on the banks of the River
Tiber, the son of Hercules and a nymph. The Fabius
whose life I am writing was slow in speaking and learning, and he entered into sports with other children only
after deliberation, so that superficial people thought him
stupid. A few saw that this tardiness sprang from sta-
bility. After he had become distinguished, people recognized that his so-called lack of energy was due to prudence and firmness. Altogether, he was consul five times.

When Hannibal invaded Italy and won a great battle

at the River Trebia and then marched through Etruria, desolating the whole countryside, terror seized Rome. In addition to the usual signs of thunder and lightning, several utterly strange portents were reported. It was said that some targets sweated blood; that at Antium, when they reaped the grain, the ears were filled with blood; that it had rained red-hot stones; and that some people had seen the heavens open and scrolls fall down, on one of which was written, "Mars, the god of war, is stirring."

None of this had any effect on Flaminius, the impetuous and fiery consul. Fabius, however, thought it a poor time to engage the enemy, not because of the prodigies, which he did not pretend to understand, but because he thought it wisest not to meet a tried general in the field; rather, he urged sending aid to Rome's allied cities and letting Hannibal waste away and expire, like a flame, for lack of sustenance. But Flaminius boldly said that he would never let any enemy advance on Rome and hastened against Hannibal, who was near Lake Trasimene in Etruria. At the moment of the battle, there was a terrible earthquake that destroyed several towns, altered the course of rivers, and carried off parts of high cliffs. But the combatants fought so fiercely that they were unaware of this.

Flaminius fell in the battle, as did the bravest of his army, to the number of 15,000; as many more were made prisoners. When the news reached Rome, the praetor called the people together and, without any attempt at disguising the gravity of affairs, said bluntly, "We have been beaten, Romans, in a great battle; the consul Flaminius has been killed; consider what must be done for your safety." This threw the city into utter confusion. At last the people decided to choose a dictator who, by his sole supreme power and by his personal wisdom and courage, might be able to manage the public affairs. Their unanimous choice fell on Fabius. His character seemed equal to the greatness of the office; his age was far enough advanced to give him experience, without taking from him the vigor of action; and his disposition was a happy mixture of confidence and caution.

When he had been installed in the office of dictator, Fabius made Lucius Minucius the master of the horse. The first solemn act of his dictatorship was very fittingly a religious one. He admonished the people that their recent defeat had not been due to lack of courage in their soldiers, but to the neglect of divine ceremonies in general. Therefore he exhorted them not to fear the enemy, but to propitiate the gods.

Having encouraged the people by making them believe that the gods were on their side, and full of confidence in himself, Fabius set forth against Hannibal. He had no intention of fighting Hannibal, but rather of wearing him out, killing stragglers and wasting his resources. Accordingly, he always camped on very high ground, where the enemy's cavalry could not attack him. When Hannibal marched, he marched; when Hannibal camped, he camped, but at enough of a distance so that there would be no engagement. He gave Hannibal no rest, but on the contrary kept his army in a state of alarm.

However, Fabius' dilatory tactics eventually made his own men suspect that he lacked courage, and the same opinion spread to Hannibal's army. Hannibal was the only person not to be deceived, for he detected the skill and tactics and saw that, unless he could bring on a battle, the resources of the Carthaginians would be ultimately drained. So, with all the arts and subtleties of war, he resolved to bring Fabius into an engagement. At one moment he would attack, to distract Fabius' attention, at another he would try to draw him off in various directions and thus tempt him from his safe policy. This had no effect at all upon the dictator, but the soldiers thought differently, and so did Minucius, the master of the horse.

Minucius was really eager for action. The common soldiers said that he was the only general worthy to command the Romans. They insolently jested that Fabius camped on the mountains, so that, as it were, they might be seated in a theater and look down on the flames and desolation of their country. But Fabius would not change his tactics.

Then Hannibal made a mistake. He wanted to refresh his horses in some good pastures, but Fabius knew the roads so well that he was able to block up the exit through the mountain pass. When Hannibal discovered the mistake he had made, he crucified the guides and then resorted to this stratagem. He ordered that torches should be fastened to the horns of 2,000 oxen in his camp. The torches were lighted at the beginning of the night, and the animals were then driven toward the heights commanding the pass, where the enemy were. This done, he ordered his army to march leisurely in the dark behind them. At first the oxen went on at a slow orderly pace, their lighted heads looking like an army marching by night. But when the fire had burned down the horns of the beasts to the quick, they no longer went along slowly, but became unruly and wild with their pain and ran about, tossing their heads and scattering fires everywhere. The Romans, who were guarding the heights, were so surprised by the flames, which seemed to come from men advancing with torches, that they fled. And thus Hannibal and his army marched safely through the pass.

Fabius discovered the trick before the night was over, for some of the oxen fell into his hands. At daybreak he attacked Hannibal in the rear, but Hannibal detached a troop of his nimble Spaniards, who were good at mountain climbing, and these quickly killed many Romans, encumbered as they were with their heavy armor. Accordingly, the Roman soldiers began to say that Fabius not only lacked courage, as they had always thought, but that he was also deficient in that generalship by which he had proposed to end the war.

To increase the anger directed at Fabius, Hannibal marched his army close to Fabius' estates and ordered his soldiers to burn the entire countryside, except for the property belonging to Fabius. When this was reported at Rome, it had the effect on the people that Hannibal desired. The magistrates, the senate, and the people were all angry with Fabius, and for various reasons. One was that Fabius had made a bargain with Hannibal to exchange prisoners, man for man, and if any remained over, they were to be ransomed at the price of 250 drachmas a head [1 drachma = 30 cents]. After this was done, there remained 240 Roman prisoners who had not been exchanged. The senate now refused to provide the money and declared that Fabius had had no right to say that he would ransom men whose cowardice had put them in the hands of the enemy. Fabius, however, was determined to keep his word with Hannibal and not to abandon the captives, and accordingly he sent his son to Rome to sell his property, and with the proceeds he ransomed them.

It was just about this time that Fabius was recalled to Rome by the priests to assist with certain official sacrifices. He left the army in the charge of Minucius, but begged him not to engage in battle with Hannibal. But no sooner had Fabius left than Minucius attacked a large detachment of the enemy and destroyed it. This filled the soldiers with rash confidence. When the news reached Rome, Fabius said that the one thing he feared most was Minucius' success, but others charged him with lack of courage and even loyalty.

Fabius announced that he would not answer the charges, but that as soon as he had finished with the sacrifices he would return to the army and punish Minucius for disobedience. A Roman dictator had this legal right, and therefore to protect Minucius the people gave him equal authority with Fabius in the conduct of the war. This was the first time that the Romans had ever divided the power of the dictatorship.

When he rejoined the army, Fabius found Minucius all puffed up with his new authority. Minucius now proposed that each of them should command on alternate days, but Fabius insisted that it was better to divide the army between them. When Hannibal heard of this new arrangement, he laid an ambush for the eager and hotheaded Minucius. His bait was swallowed whole by Minucius, who now found himself surrounded by the Carthaginians. In particular, the Numidian cavalry roamed everywhere and slaughtered the Romans. Fabius had suspected that some such disaster as this would befall Minucius, and therefore he had held himself in watchful reserve. At the critical moment he came to Minucius' rescue and drove Hannibal off. Minucius threw himself into the arms of the dictator and saluted not only his military ability, but his wisdom which now, at last, was clear.

The appointed time now arrived for Fabius to lay down his dictatorship, and consuls were again elected. At first, the new consuls followed Fabius' policy and avoided a

pitched battle with Hannibal. But then Terentius Varro
was elected consul. He was a man of obscure birth, but
his boldness made him popular. With a rash ignorance he
said that he would stake Rome's fate on a single battle;
he explained there would never be an end to the war as
long as Rome employed generals like Fabius; and that if
he could just catch a glimpse of the enemy, he would on
that day free Italy of the foreigners. Consequently he was
able to raise the largest army that had ever been sent out
of Rome. It had no less than 88,000 fighting men. Wiser
and more experienced persons at Rome, such as Fabius,
feared what might happen if the flower of its youth
should be destroyed. They therefore explained the whole
situation to the other consul, Aemilius Paulus, a man
greatly experienced in war but not very popular with the
people.

When Varro and Paulus joined the army, it was agreed
that each should command on alternate days. Varro, on
his day, posted the army at a village called Cannae. Just
as soon as it was light, he flew the scarlet flag over his tent
which was the signal for battle. The Carthaginians were
startled by this boldness and also by the fact that the
Roman army was twice as large as theirs. Hannibal at
once made a survey of the Roman arrangements and then
employed some of his stratagems which were always so
advantageous to himself.

In the first place, Hannibal drew up his men so that
the wind was at their backs. The wind was blowing

violently that day over the sandy plain, and now of course the clouds of dust would blow into the faces of the Romans. Next, he placed all his best men on the two wings; the center of his army he drew up so that it projected in front of the two wings, but the worst soldiers were placed here. He explained to the men on the wings that the Roman attack would be directed at their center, and that inevitably the center would be forced to recoil before the shock. This meant that the Romans would push on in the center, pursuing their foe, but when they had gone far enough in, then the wings should attack. This, he said, would take the Romans on the flank, and they would be surrounded. And that is exactly what happened. Over 50,000 Romans were killed in the battle, including Aemilius Paulus. Thousands were taken prisoner. Varro and a few others managed to escape.

Hannibal's friends now urged him to attack Rome, but, either because of divine intervention or because he knew it was impossible to take the city without the siege machinery that he lacked, he did not. A Carthaginian said to him with some indignation, "You know how to win a victory, Hannibal, but not how to use it." Nevertheless, Hannibal's affairs now prospered wonderfully, as one city after another, such as Capua and Tarentum, declared for him.

The people at Rome recognized that what they had branded as cowardice and fear on the part of Fabius had actually been wisdom. Amid the general mourning and confusion, Fabius now walked the streets with a confident air, spoke cheerfully to his fellow citizens, and checked the lamentations of the women. He told the senate and the magistrates what must be done for the city's safety, and at the gates he placed guards to keep the frightened multitude from fleeing.

Let us now speak in admiration of the high spirit of this Roman state. When the consul Varro came back after Cannae, full of shame and humiliation, the whole senate and people met him at the gates with honor and respect. On their behalf, Fabius commended him, because he did not despair of the safety of the state, but had returned to execute the laws.

The Romans now sent out more generals against Hannibal, Fabius among them. Fabius pursued the same tactics as before, but in addition he was able to capture the important city of Tarentum, which had revolted from Rome earlier. In honor of this, the Romans decreed him a triumph, much more splendid than his first.

The Romans took an important step when, next, they sent the young Publius Cornelius Scipio to Spain, which Hannibal was using as a base. Scipio was everywhere victorious against the Carthaginians, and on his return to Rome was elected to the consulship. His new plan was to transfer the war to Africa and in this way compel the Carthaginians to recall Hannibal from Italy. Fabius, in his cautious manner, vigorously opposed the idea, but nonetheless Scipio departed for Africa with his forces.

He won great victories at once, and the Carthaginians were indeed compelled to order Hannibal home. Not long afterward, at Zama, Scipio utterly defeated Hannibal and humbled the pride of Carthage.

The Romans were overwhelmed with joy, but Fabius did not live to see the victory. About the time that Hannibal left Italy, he fell sick and died. Although there was no need of it, the Romans, as a mark of their affection, defrayed the cost of his funeral by contributing, each of them, a small coin. Thus they claimed Fabius as their common father and made his end no less honorable than his life.

CATO THE ELDER

(234–149 B.C. Marcus Porcius Cato the Elder—sometimes called Cato the Censor—was the outstanding example of Rome's ancient simple virtues; this at a time when, after the defeat of Hannibal, foreign influences were pouring in on Rome. In particular, Cato feared Greek refinement. In his book on agriculture, Cato gave meticulous advice about the growing of vineyards, vegetables, and so on, and explained how to treat slaves: work them hard as long as they are healthy and then turn them out to live or die. The reviving prosperity of Carthage alarmed Cato and, though he did not live to see the obliteration of Carthage in 146 B.C., he was instrumental in bringing on the Third Punic War: for years he ended every speech in the senate, no matter what its subject, with the words, "Carthage must be destroyed.")

Cato was born at Tusculum, although he was brought up in the country of the Sabines, where his father's farm was situated. He often spoke in praise of his great-grandfather, who lost no less than five horses under him in battle.

Cato had a ruddy complexion and gray eyes which, some people said, could actually snarl at you. From his youth he worked with his hands, lived temperately, and served in war. He especially practiced oratory, which he knew was the way to rise above a humble existence. When eventually he became a good pleader, or lawyer, he would not take any fee, for the only combats that counted, so he would say, were real battles.

At the age of seventeen, when Hannibal was pillaging Italy, Cato made his first campaign and got his chest all covered with scars. In battle he would strike boldly, never retreating an inch, and would fix his stern countenance on his enemy and accost him threateningly, thinking this kind of behavior as terrifying as his sword. He always carried his own arms on an expedition, went on foot, and brought along only one servant. He would often help prepare his supper and, as a rule, drank only water. If he was very thirsty, he might mix a little vinegar with the water and, in case of fatigue, take some wine.

The little cottage of Manius Curius, who had thrice won a triumph, happened to be near Cato's farm. Cato would often go there and consider its small size and plainness and then reflect that it had belonged to one of Rome's great military heroes. It was here that Manius had received the Samnite envoys, who found him boiling turnips in the corner of the chimney. And when the Samnites tried to make him a present of gold, Manius refused it, saying that it was more honorable to conquer those who possessed the gold than to possess the gold itself. When he had thought about such things, Cato would return to his farm, increase his own work, and cut down on all superfluous expenses.

Cato served under Fabius Maximus at the time Tarentum was recaptured from Hannibal. He learned from his tentmate something about the ideas of the Greek philosopher, Plato; for example, that pleasure is evil's chief bait and that the body is the principal calamity of the soul. But he refused to study Greek until he was an old man.

A very influential Roman, Valerius Flaccus by name, happened to live near Cato. Flaccus was the kind of person who can recognize excellence in a youth. He admired the way Cato would work with his hands, go on foot to the courts in the morning and back again in the evening, eat with his servants, and act moderately. Accordingly, he urged Cato to apply himself to state business in Rome. Thus, with the help of Flaccus, Cato rose to be consul and even censor. Among the older senators, it was Fabius Maximus to whom Cato especially attached himself, so that he might have constantly before him the example of his life. But he opposed himself to the great Scipio, because of his extravagant way of living.

Cato became more and more powerful at Rome as his eloquence developed, but he was even more famous for his manner of living. For now Rome had become great and could not maintain the pure and simple ways of the past. Foreigners and foreign customs penetrated the city. Therefore, when others were giving themselves over to pleasures and growing effeminate, they saw Cato maintain his ways right into old age. Cato says that he never wore a suit of clothes that cost more than a hundred drachmas [1 drachma = 30 cents] and that, when he was consul, he drank the same wine as his workmen; nor did he ever plaster any of his farmhouses. Slaves, he said, should be sold when they grow old, and no useless servants should be fed.

Some people put these things down to avarice. As for myself, I think it wrong to treat slaves like beasts, turning them out and selling them in their old age. Kindness and humanity demand more than mere justice. We cannot use living creatures like old shoes or dishes, and throw them away when they are worn out.

Cato, however, deserves our highest admiration for his self-control as general and provincial governor. When he became governor of Sardinia, he found that his predecessors always charged the state for tents, bedding, and clothes, to say nothing of their entertainments. Cato's economy was hardly credible. He walked without a carriage to visit the cities, with one companion to carry his official dress and libation cup. Though he spared those who were under his power, he showed an inflexible strictness in the administration of justice. The result was that the Roman government never seemed more terrible, nor yet more mild, than under his administration.

Cato used to say that in his whole life he repented of only three things: one was that he had trusted a secret to a woman; another, that he had once traveled by water when he could have gone by land; and the third was that he had spent one whole day without doing any important business. Unlike some people, I feel that a man's character comes out more clearly in his words than in his looks.

Cato performed distinguished military service in Spain and later in Greece against Antiochus the Great who, next to Hannibal, struck more terror into the Romans than any other enemy. As for his civil policy, Cato held that a chief duty was to accuse and jail criminals. His harshness made his enemies eager to find him at fault somewhere. He was sued fifty times during his life; the last occasion was when he was eighty-five years old and made his memorable remark that it was hard for him, who had lived with one generation of men, to plead now before another.

Ten years after his consulship, Cato stood for the office of censor. This office is the summit of all honor at Rome. Besides his other power, the censor can inquire into anyone's life and manners. The Romans therefore chose two persons as censor. These officials could take away a man's horse or expel him from the senate, if he lived intemperately. It was their business to estimate every man's wealth and to register his birth and station. The nobility feared Cato's austerity and put seven men up to oppose him. They promised the people all kinds of favors, as if all they wanted was an easy government. Cato promised no such mildness and threatened all those who lived extravagantly. The Roman people were so worthy of great leaders, however, that they elected Cato and Valerius Flaccus, who had been a candidate with him.

As censor, Cato expelled from the senate various individuals, some of them well known, for their manner of living. For example, one person, who was scheduled to be consul the following year, he removed from the senate because he had kissed his wife in the presence of his daughter and in broad daylight. Cato's actions, of course, made him unpopular, but it was his cutting down on luxury in general that caused particular annoyance. This was a difficult thing for him to do, since so many people had already been corrupted by riches. His method was to tax at ten times their value such things as dress carriages, women's ornaments, and fancy furniture. People were disgusted with Cato for, as a rule, they seem to think that an order not to show off one's riches is equivalent to taking them away. The desire for ostentatious wealth does not spring from a natural passion within us, but from the vulgar opinion of others.

Another reason for Cato's unpopularity was that, in letting out contracts for public works, he beat down the bids and awarded the contracts to the lowest bidder. The common people, however, liked Cato's censorship. When they set up a statue in his honor, the inscription on it did not refer to his military triumphs, but simply to the fact that this was Cato the Censor, who, by his discipline and temperance, kept the Roman state from sinking into vice.

Cato was a good father and an excellent husband. The woman he married was noble rather than rich, for he believed that the rich are haughty, whereas the noble despise base things and are more ready to obey their husbands in whatever is proper. His wife nursed their son herself. And as the boy grew up, Cato taught him to read, being unwilling to leave this to his servant, who was, however, an excellent grammarian. Cato also instructed the boy in law and in his gymnastic exercises; he showed him how to shoot arrows, to fight in armor, to ride and box and swim. Moreover, he wrote histories, so that the boy could learn about his country and ancestors without stirring from the house.

When some famous Greek philosophers arrived in Rome with certain requests, Cato opposed them, for he saw the youth flocking around them and decided that the young might come to value the glory of speaking more than that of bearing arms. On the whole, he despised philosophy and in particular scoffed at Greek studies and literature. For example, he would say that Socrates, the great Athenian philosopher, was a prating, seditious fellow, who tried to tyrannize his country and undermine the ancient customs by enticing the citizens to hold opinions contrary to the laws. He pronounced, as if he were an oracle, that the Romans would surely be destroyed when they fell in love with Greek literature, although, of course, the passage of time has shown that Rome rose to its height of good fortune when it embraced Greek learning.

Some people maintain that the final overthrow of Carthage was due to Cato. The reviving power and wealth of Carthage, since the defeat of Hannibal, frightened him, and he said so to the senate. Once he showed the senators some ripe African figs, which, he declared, had been picked in a place only three days' sail from Rome. Therefore, he ended every speech in the senate with the words, "Carthage must be destroyed."

And so Cato stirred up the third and last war against the Carthaginians. But no sooner had the war begun than he died. It was his great-grandson, Cato the Younger, an illustrious philosopher and opponent of Julius Caesar, who a century later committed suicide at Utica, in Africa, when he considered that the cause of freedom had been lost.

JULIUS CAESAR

(100–44 B.C. A military genius, Gaius Julius Caesar conquered Gaul; after his defeat of Pompey, he became master of the Roman world and by his reforms proved himself a great statesman as well. The ultimate result of Caesar's Gallic wars was the civilizing of western Europe; immediately, however, he showed that the possession of a trained army could lead to personal dominion. His murder merely postponed the formal demise of the Roman Republic and the establishment of the Empire.)

Caesar's second wife was Cornelia, the daughter of Rome's late dictator, Cinna. When Sulla became dictator of Rome, he tried to get Caesar to divorce his wife, but could not, so he contented himself with confiscating her dowry. The reason Sulla hated Caesar was because Caesar was related to Marius, his enemy. In the beginning of his rule, Sulla put many people to death; when some persons urged him to spare Caesar, who was only a youth, he said that they had no sense if they could not see many Mariuses in that boy.

When this was reported to Caesar, he slipped off to sea and sailed for Bithynia in Asia Minor. Subsequently, he was captured by some pirates, for their fleets infested the seas everywhere. These men demanded twenty talents for his ransom [1 talent = $1,800], but Caesar laughed at them for not understanding the value of their prisoner and promised them fifty. He sent most of his companions away to raise the money, so that he was left with only a couple of friends among the Cilicians, who are the most bloodthirsty men in the world. Caesar held them in such contempt, however, that, when he wished to sleep, he told them to keep quiet. For thirty-eight days he was completely free and joined in their exercises and games. He wrote poems and speeches and read them to the pirates, and if they did not admire them, he would call them illiterate and threaten to hang them. The pirates put this down as a kind of simplicity and boyish playfulness.

When the ransom arrived from Miletus, Caesar paid it and immediately went to Miletus and procured some ships. He then pursued the pirates, captured most of them and recovered his money. He took ten pirates up to Pergamum, where he had them crucified—a punishment he had often threatened them with while he was in their hands, though they little dreamed he was in earnest.

Meanwhile, Sulla's power began to decline, and Caesar's friends urged him to return to Rome. Instead, he went to Rhodes and entered the school of Apollonius, a famous rhetorician who once had Cicero as a pupil. Caesar is said to have been admirably fitted by nature to make a great statesman and orator, and he worked hard so that he might at least be second in such matters. More than that he did not aim at, for he chose rather to be first among men of arms and power. Therefore, he never rose to that height of eloquence to which nature would have carried him, his attention being riveted on the expeditions and schemes which at length gained him the Roman Empire.

Caesar found, on his return to Rome, that his eloquence won him great credit and favor, particularly among the common people. The open house he kept, the entertainments he gave, and the general splendor of his life contributed, little by little, to increase his political influence. His enemies slighted this at first, supposing that he would fail when his money was gone. When at last his power was established and was aimed openly at altering the whole constitution of the state, they were aware too late that there is no beginning so small which continued application will not make great. Cicero was the first to suspect Caesar's designs on the government, for he could detect under Caesar's good humor the ambition for absolute power. "And yet," said Cicero, "when I see his hair so carefully arranged, and observe him adjusting it with one finger, I cannot imagine it should enter into such a man's thoughts to overthrow the Roman government." More on this later, however.

The first proof Caesar had of the people's good will was when they elected him to a tribuneship in the army. A second and clearer instance of their favor was on the

occasion of the funeral of his Aunt Julia, the wife of
Marius, when he praised her openly in the Forum and
boldly exhibited images of Marius—something no one
had dared to do after the government came into Sulla's
hands, for Marius' party was declared an enemy of the
state. A few people cried out against Caesar when he did
this, but most of the people shouted in his favor. Moreover, it had always been the custom at Rome to make
funeral orations in praise of elderly women, but there
was no precedent for an oration on a young woman until
Caesar first made one on the death of his own wife. This
also won him favor with the people, who regarded him
as a man of great kindness and tenderness of heart.

After the funeral of his wife, Caesar went as quaestor
to Spain. When this duty ended, he married Pompeia,
his third wife. Now Caesar spent so much money that,
even before he held any public office, he was in debt to
the tune of 1,300 talents; what he was actually doing was
to purchase, at a relatively low cost, something of the
highest value—votes. For example, when he was aedile,
he provided such a number of gladiators that he entertained the people with 320 single combats. By his magnificence in theatrical shows, in processions and public
banquets, he put into the shade all such things as had
been done before him. Accordingly, the people were eager
to reward him with new offices and honors.

Caesar met with a misfortune in his domestic affairs
during his praetorship. There was a certain patrician,

Publius Clodius by name, who was eminent for his riches and eloquence, but in the licentiousness of his life he exceeded the most noted profligates of the day. He was in love with Pompeia, Caesar's wife, and she seemed not to object. But a strict watch was kept on her apartment, and Caesar's mother, Aurelia, was continually around her, so that any interview was difficult.

Well, the Romans have a goddess whom they call Bona. The Greeks say she is the mother of the Dionysus whose name is not to be uttered. For this reason the women who celebrate her festival cover the tents with vine branches and, in accordance with the myth, a sacred serpent is placed beside the goddess. It is not lawful for any man to be nearby, not even in the house, while the rites are being celebrated; but the women themselves perform the sacred offices, which are reputedly much the same as those used in the rites of Orpheus. At the time of the festival, the husband and all men leave the house; the wife sets everything in order. The principal ceremonies are performed during the night, the women playing among themselves as they keep watch, and music is played.

At this particular time, when Pompeia was celebrating the festival, Clodius did not yet have a beard, and so he thought he might pass undiscovered. He put on the dress and ornaments of a singing woman and went to Pompeia's house, as if he were a young girl. Finding the doors open, he was admitted by the maid, who was in on the secret and promptly ran to tell Pompeia. But as she was away a long time, Clodius became uneasy and started going through the house, taking care to avoid the lights. At last Aurelia's woman met him and invited him to play with her, as the women did among themselves. When he refused, she pulled him forward and asked him about himself. Clodius told her he was waiting for Pompeia's own maid, Abra, and as he spoke, he betrayed himself by his voice.

Upon this the woman shrieked and ran into the company where there were lights, crying that she had discovered a man. The women were all frightened. Aurelia covered up the sacred things and stopped the proceedings. Then, ordering the doors to be locked, she went about with lights and found Clodius hiding in the maid's room. The women knew him and drove him out of doors and at once, that same night, went home and told their husbands the story.

In the morning it was all over town, what an impious attempt Clodius had made, and how he ought to be punished for having offended the public and the gods. Thereupon one of the tribunes impeached him for profaning holy rites, and the principal senators gave evidence against some of his other crimes. But the people set themselves against this combination of the nobility and defended Clodius; this helped him with the judges, who were afraid to provoke the multitude. Caesar at once divorced Pompeia, but when he was summoned as a witness against Clodius, he said he had nothing to charge him with. This struck the accuser as a paradox, and he asked Caesar why, in that case, he had divorced his wife. "Because," Caesar replied, "I wished my wife to be above suspicion."

After his praetorship, Caesar was appointed governor of the province of Spain, but as he was about to set off, his creditors pressed him for payment. This led him to apply to Crassus, who was the richest man in Rome, but was politically ambitious and needed Caesar's youthful vigor against Pompey. Crassus paid off the most pressing creditors and pledged himself to the amount of 830 talents, whereupon Caesar was able to go to his province. He managed the military and civil affairs of Spain well and left with a fair reputation, having enriched both himself and his soldiers, to boot.

On his return to Rome, Caesar decided to stand for the consulship. He now followed a policy that deceived everyone except Cato the Younger—namely, the reconciling of Crassus and Pompey, the two most powerful men in Rome, who had quarreled. Thus he strengthened himself by the united power of both; and, under cover of what seemed to be a kindly action, he caused what was, in effect, a revolution in the government. For it was not the quarrel between Pompey and Caesar, as most men imagine, which was the origin of the civil wars, but

their union, their conspiring together, at first, to overthrow the aristocracy and then quarreling afterward between themselves.

And so, with the support of Crassus and Pompey, Caesar was elected to the consulship with Calpurnius Bibulus
as colleague. When he entered on the office, Caesar proposed bold bills, such as the foundation of colonies and
the division of property, simply to please the people. The
most honorable senators opposed him, whereupon Caesar
said that the senate's insulting conduct left him with no
alternative but to devote himself henceforth to the popular cause.

In order to get a yet firmer hold upon Pompey, Caesar betrothed his daughter Julia to him, and then married
Calpurnia, the daughter of Piso. He made Piso consul
for the next year. This made Cato protest that it was in-
tolerable that the government should be prostituted by
marriages and that they should advance one another to
the commands of armies, provinces, and other great posts,
by means of women.

Bibulus, Caesar's colleague, finding that he could not
oppose Caesar's bills, but that he was in danger of being
murdered in the Forum, as was Cato too, shut himself up
in his house and there spent the remaining part of his
consulship. Pompey, as soon as he was married, filled
the Forum with soldiers and gave the people his help in
passing the new laws. He also won for Caesar the con-
sular province of Gaul, both on this side of the Alps and

on the other side, together with Illyricum, and the command of four legions for five long years.

Thus far we have followed Caesar's actions before the wars in Gaul. After this, he seems to begin his career afresh and to enter upon a new life and scene of action. And the period of those wars which he now fought, and those many expeditions in which he subdued Gaul, showed him to be a soldier and general not in the least inferior to any of the greatest commanders who have ever appeared at the head of armies. The difficulty and extent of the country he subdued; the number and strength of the enemy he defeated; the wildness and perfidiousness of the tribes and his good will toward them; his clemency to the conquered, his gifts and kindnesses to his soldiers— what other general in history can match this? During the ten years he ultimately spent in Gaul, he captured 800 towns, subdued 300 states, and, of the three million men who opposed him, he killed one million and captured another million.

Caesar inspired his men with his own love of honor and passion for distinction. By generously distributing money and honors he showed that he was not heaping up wealth from the wars for his own luxury, but that it was a reward for valor. Moreover, there was no danger to which he did not willingly expose himself, no labor from which he shrank. Although the soldiers were not mystified by his contempt of danger, because they knew how

much he coveted honor, they were astonished by his en-
during so much hardship beyond his natural strength.
For Caesar was of a slight build, had a soft and white
skin, and was subject to epilepsy. However, he did not
make his bodily weakness a pretext for ease, but rather
used war as the best possible medicine; by fatiguing jour-
neys, simple diet, frequent sleeping outdoors, and continual exercise, he fortified his body against all attacks.
He slept generally in his chariots or while he was carried
in a litter. In the daytime he was thus carried to forts,
garrisons, and camps, one servant sitting with him, who
used to write down what he dictated as he went. He drove
so rapidly that when he left Rome he arrived at the River
Rhone in eight days.

Caesar's first campaign in Gaul was against the Helvetians and Tigurini who, having burned their towns,
planned to march through that part of Gaul which was
included in the Roman province, just as the Cimbri and
Teutons had once done. There were 300,000 of them, of
whom 190,000 were fighting men. Caesar sent his famous officer, Labienus, against the Tigurini; he routed
them near the River Arar. As for the Helvetians, Caesar
had to fight against them even among their wagons,
where the women and children defended themselves till
they were cut to pieces. Caesar gathered all the survivors,
some 100,000, and forced them to reoccupy the country
they had deserted and the cities they had burned. He did

this for fear the Germans would possess the land if it lay uninhabited.

Caesar next fought in defense of the Gauls against the Germans. Their king, Ariovistus, was actually his ally, but Caesar saw that at the first chance they would try to occupy Gaul. Some of his young officers, who had come along in the hope of winning glory and wealth, were a bit timid about this campaign, but the famous tenth legion responded so enthusiastically that all followed with zeal.

Ariovistus never expected Caesar to attack the Germans. Moreover, at this moment, they were discouraged by the prophecies of their holy women, who foretell the future by observing the eddies of rivers and by noting the windings and noise of streams. These women now warned the Germans not to fight until the next new moon. When Caesar learned of this, he decided that this was just the time to attack them. He killed many of the enemy and pursued them as far as the River Rhine. Ariovistus fled across the Rhine with the remnants of his army, leaving 80,000 dead behind.

Caesar then stationed his army in winter quarters among the Sequani and, in order to attend to his affairs at Rome, went to that part of Gaul which lies on the River Po and was part of his province. South of the Po is the Rubicon, and it is the latter river which divides Gaul on this side of the Alps, as it is called, from the rest of Italy [it would have been treason for a general with troops to cross the Rubicon into Italy proper]. Great numbers of people came to see Caesar, and he sent all away with gifts and favors and promises about the future.

News now reached Caesar that the Belgae, who were the most powerful of all the Gauls and inhabited a third of the country, had revolted. He hastened against them and quickly subdued them and the Nervii. In fact, out of 60,000 Nervii, it is said that not over 500 survived the battle. When the Roman senate heard of this, it voted sacrifices and festivals to the gods for a period of fifteen days, longer than had ever been observed for any victory before.

Caesar himself, after settling the affairs in Gaul, came back and spent the winter by the Po, in order to carry out his plans at Rome. He gave money to his candidates for office, so that they could corrupt the people and buy their votes and then, when elected, advance his own power. More significant was the fact that the most powerful men in Rome came to see him at Luca, among them Pompey and Crassus, and in all about 200 senators. It was decided at Luca that Pompey and Crassus should be consuls the next year, and that Caesar's command in Gaul should be extended for another five years.

After this, Caesar returned to Gaul, where he found that German tribes had crossed the Rhine and stirred up revolts. So Caesar made this a pretext for invading the land of the Germans, being ambitious to be the first man to cross the Rhine with an army. He built a bridge across the river, though it was wide at this point, and the current was swift and dashed trunks of trees against the foundations of the bridge. Caesar, however, drove great piles of wood into the bottom of the river just above the bridge, and these caught the trees and other things floating down and thus protected the bridge.

The bridge was completed in ten days. The Suevi, who are the most warlike people in all Germany, fled before his approach. After he had burned the countryside, Caesar returned to Gaul eighteen days later.

Caesar's expedition to Britain was the most famous example of his courage. He was the first who brought a navy into the western ocean, or who sailed into the Atlantic with an army to make war. Historians had actually doubted the existence of the island, considering it a mere name or piece of fiction, and so Caesar may be said to have carried the Roman Empire beyond the limits of the known world. He crossed twice from Gaul and fought several battles. But he did not win much for himself, since the islanders were very poor. Accordingly, he took hostages from the king and, after imposing a tribute, left Britain.

Back in Gaul, Caesar received letters announcing that his daughter Julia, Pompey's wife, had died in childbirth; soon afterward the child also died. Both Caesar and Pompey were much affected by Julia's death; as were also their friends, for they felt that the alliance was broken which had kept the troubled state in peace.

Caesar's troops were now so numerous that he had to distribute them in various camps for winter quarters. Then, according to custom, he went to Italy. Scattered revolts brought him back soon to Gaul; and, in the course of the winter, he visited every part of the country. But, after a while, the seeds of war, which had long since been secretly sown by the most powerful men in those warlike nations, broke forth into the greatest and most dangerous war that was ever fought there. More men had gathered for it, youthful and vigorous and well armed; they had much money; their towns were strongly fortified. Besides, it was winter, and the rivers were frozen, the woods were covered with snow, paths were obliterated, and there were overflowing marshes. It seemed unlikely, therefore, that Caesar would march against the rebels. The general who was in supreme command of the rebels was Vercingetorix, chief of the Arverni.

But Caesar was gifted above all other men with the faculty of making the right use of everything in war, and especially in seizing the right moment. Therefore, as soon as he heard of the revolt, he advanced quickly in the terrible weather with his army. In fact, in the time that it would have taken an ordinary messenger to cover the distance, Caesar appeared with all his army, ravaged the country, reduced outposts, and captured towns.

Even the Aedui, who had hitherto been friends of the Roman people and had been honored by them, joined the rebels. Accordingly Caesar struck out for the land of the

Sequani, who were his friends. At this point tens of thousands of the enemy set upon him, but after much slaughter he won a victory.

The rest of the enemy fled with Vercingetorix into a town called Alesia. Caesar besieged it, though the height of the walls and the number of defenders made it appear impregnable. Then suddenly, from outside the walls, Caesar was assailed by a greater danger than can be described. For the best men of Gaul, picked out of each nation, and well armed, came to the relief of Alesia. There were 300,000 of these men, and inside the town were 170,000 more. And so Caesar was shut up between the two forces. He now built two walls, one toward the town, and the other against the relieving army, for he knew that he would be ruined if the enemy joined forces.

The danger that Caesar underwent at Alesia justly gained him great honor and gave him the opportunity of showing his valor as no other contest had done. But it seems extraordinary that he was able to defeat thousands of men outside the town without those inside being able to see it. Even the Romans guarding the wall next to the town did not know of it, until finally they heard the cries of the men and women inside who spied the Roman soldiers carrying into their camp great quantities of shields adorned with gold and silver, and breastplates stained with blood, besides cups and tents made in the Gallic fashion. Just as fast as that did a vast army vanish like a ghost or dream, most of them being killed on the spot.

At last those who were in Alesia surrendered. Vercingetorix put on his best armor, adorned his horse, and rode out of the gates to Caesar; then he dismounted and threw off his armor and remained quietly sitting at Caesar's feet until he was led away for the triumph in Rome.

Caesar had long ago resolved upon Pompey's overthrow, as had Pompey, for that matter, on his. The fear of Crassus had kept them in peace, but Crassus had recently been killed by the Parthians. And so, if one of them wished to make himself the greatest man in Rome, he had only to overthrow the other.

Rome itself was now the scene of election riots and murders. Some thought that the only hope lay in monarchy. Others tried to reconcile Pompey and Caesar, but they would not yield, and finally two of Caesar's friends —Antony and Curio—were driven out of the senate house with insults. This gave Caesar the chance to inflame his soldiers, for he showed them two reputable Romans of authority who had been forced to escape in a hired wagon dressed as slaves.

Caesar was now in Gaul on this side of the Alps, with 300 cavalry and 5,000 infantry; the rest of his army was beyond the Alps with orders to follow. But Caesar felt that here, at the beginning of his design, he did not need large forces; he planned, rather, to astound his enemies with the speed and boldness of his plan. This particular day he spent in public as a spectator of gladiatorial games. Then, a little before night, he dressed and went into the hall and chatted for some time with those he had invited to supper. When it began to grow dark, he rose from the table and made his excuses to the company. Then he and a few friends drove off in hired wagons, some going one way and some another—so that no one could suspect what they were up to—until at last he came to the River Rubicon which, as I have said, divides Cisalpine Gaul from the rest of Italy.

Caesar now began to reflect upon the danger, and he wavered when he considered the greatness of the enterprise. He checked himself and halted, while he turned things over in his mind. He discussed the matter at some length with Asinius Pollio and other friends who were with him, estimating how many calamities his passing of that small river would bring on mankind, and what a tale about it would be transmitted to posterity. At last, in a sort of passion, throwing aside calculation and abandoning himself to what might come, he used the proverb of people entering upon dangerous attempts, "The die is cast," and crossed the river. He then pushed south as fast as possible.

Wide gates, so to speak, were now thrown open to let in war upon every land and sea. Men and women fled, in their consternation, from one town of Italy to another. The city of Rome was overrun with a deluge of people flying in from all the neighboring places. Magistrates could no longer govern, nor could the eloquence of an orator quiet the mob.

Pompey at this time had more forces than Caesar. But he did not think clearly and believed false reports that Caesar was close at hand. He was carried away by the general panic. And so he issued an edict that the city was in a state of anarchy and left it, ordering the senators to follow him unless they preferred tyranny to their country and liberty. Even Labienus, who had been one of Caesar's best officers and friends and had fought zealously in the Gallic wars, now deserted him and went over to Pompey. Thereupon Caesar sent Labienus his money and baggage.

Pompey fled south all the way to Brundisium and shipped the consuls and soldiers across the Adriatic Sea to Dyrrachium. He himself soon followed, on Caesar's approach. But Caesar could not pursue him, since he had no boats, and therefore turned back to Rome. He had made himself master of all Italy, without bloodshed, in sixty days.

Caesar arranged things in Rome and then went off to Spain, so that no enemy would be left behind him when he marched against Pompey. Back in Rome, he stopped only briefly and then hastened with all speed to Brundisium. It was the beginning of January and the winter storms made it difficult for him to transport his troops across the Adriatic. Finally this was done, and Caesar was joined by Antony and other friends. After several skirmishes, both Pompey and Caesar moved their armies into Greece.

The two armies now encamped at Pharsalus, in Thessaly. Pompey was still against fighting, because of certain omens. His friends, on the other hand, acted as if they had already won the battle, and some even sent messages to Rome to rent houses for them fit for consuls and praetors, so sure were they of themselves. The cavalry were especially anxious to fight, being splendidly armed and mounted on fine horses; also, they numbered 7,000 to Caesar's 1,000. Similarly, Pompey had 45,000 infantry to Caesar's 22,000.

Caesar collected together his soldiers and told them that reinforcements were on the way, but they called out to him not to wait. As soon as the sacrifices had been made to the gods, the seer told him that within three days he would come to a decisive action. Caesar asked him whether he saw anything in the entrails which promised a happy event. "That," said the seer, "you can best answer yourself; for the gods signify a great change in your affairs. If, therefore, you think yourself well off now, expect worse fortune; if unhappy, hope for the better." And the night before the battle, as Caesar was making the rounds about midnight, there was a light seen in the heavens, very bright and flaming, which seemed to pass over Caesar's camp and fall into Pompey's. In the morning Caesar's soldiers saw panic among the enemy.

Caesar now arranged his army in battle formation,
dividing it into three groups. In command of the center
he placed Calvinus. Antony commanded the left wing,
and Caesar himself the right, being resolved to fight at
the head of his tenth legion. When Caesar saw the
enemy's cavalry lining up against him, he was struck by
their fine appearance and number. Accordingly, he ordered six cohorts of infantry to come up from the rear of
his army and station themselves behind the right wing;
he gave them special instructions concerning what they
were to do when the enemy's cavalry charged, as will be
clear later.

Pompey, for his part, commanded the right wing,
Domitius the left, and Scipio (Pompey's father-in-law)
the center. The whole mass of the cavalry was stationed
on the left wing, the idea being that it should outflank
the enemy's right wing and thus rout the very part that
Caesar himself commanded. Pompey was sure that no
body of infantry could sustain such a shock, but would
be shattered to pieces by the onset of so immense a force
of cavalry.

The signal for battle was now given on both sides.
Pompey ordered the infantry to stand their ground and
not break their order, but receive the enemy's first attack, till they came within a javelin's throw. Caesar, in
his own writings, blames Pompey's generalship in this
regard: Pompey should have realized, says Caesar, how
the first encounter, when made on the run, gives weight

to the blows and actually fires the men's spirits into a
flame.

Caesar himself was just putting his troops into motion
and advancing into the action, when he found one of his
centurions, an experienced officer, encouraging his men
to the utmost. Caesar called him by name and said,
"What hopes, Gaius Crassinius, and what grounds for
encouragement?" Crassinius stretched out his hand and
yelled, "We shall conquer, Caesar; and this day, dead or
alive, I will deserve your praise." Then he charged the
enemy, followed by the 120 men of his company. He
broke through their first rank, pressed on, killing the
enemy, till at last he was hit by a sword that went in at
his mouth and came out at his neck behind.

While the infantry was thus engaged on the flank,
Pompey's cavalry rode up confidently and opened their
ranks wide, so that they could surround Caesar's right
wing. At this very moment, Caesar's cohorts—those six
cohorts of infantry which he had moved up from the rear
and had stationed behind his right wing—rushed out
and attacked the cavalry. They now followed the special
instructions which, as I have said, Caesar had given them.
This was that they were not to throw their javelins from
a distance nor were they to strike at the legs and thighs
of the enemy. They must aim at their faces. Caesar had
noted that most of Pompey's men were young, not accustomed to battles and wounds; they were naturally
vain, being in the flower of their youth, and would not

wish to risk either death now or a scar for the future. And that is the way it worked out. For Pompey's cavalry could not stand the sight of the javelins, but turned and covered their faces. Now in disorder, they fled and ruined everything. With Pompey's cavalry beaten back, Caesar's men outflanked the infantry and cut it to pieces.

When Pompey, who was commanding the other wing of his army, saw the cavalry broken and fleeing, he was no longer himself. He forgot that he was Pompey the Great and, like someone whom the gods have deprived of his senses, retired to his tent. He did not say a word, but just sat there, until his whole army was routed and the enemy appeared upon the defenses which had been thrown up before his camp. Then he seemed to recover his senses, and with the words, "What, are they in the camp too?" he took off his general's uniform and put on ordinary clothes. He then stole off and made his way to Egypt.

There were many portents that foretold this victory, but the most remarkable occurred at Tralles, in Asia Minor. The temple of Victory there contained a statue of Caesar. Naturally, the ground on which the statue stood was hard, and the stone with which it was paved harder still. And yet it is said that a palm tree actually shot up near the pedestal of Caesar's statue.

After the victory Caesar pardoned his opponents, including Brutus who afterward killed him. He then set off in pursuit of Pompey, but when he reached Alexandria, in Egypt, he learned that Potheinus—a eunuch who stood in high favor with the King of Egypt—had murdered Pompey. This caused Caesar to weep for, as he wrote friends in Rome, his greatest desire was always to save the lives of fellow citizens who had fought against him.

A war of sorts soon developed in Egypt, which was brought on by Caesar's passion for Cleopatra. Potheinus had banished her and was secretly plotting Caesar's destruction. When Caesar heard of this, he used to sit up whole nights, under the pretense of drinking, to protect himself. Moreover, Potheinus was openly insulting. He gave Caesar's soldiers moldy grain and said they must be content with it, since they were being fed at another's cost.

Caesar made it clear that he did not want Egyptians to be his counselors and secretly ordered Cleopatra to return. Accordingly, she took a small boat with just one person—a Sicilian Greek named Apollodorus—and landed at dusk near the palace. She did not know how to get in unseen, until she hit on the idea of stretching out on a blanket. Apollodorus bundled her up and carried her on his back to Caesar's apartment. Caesar was captivated by her boldness and altogether overcome by the charm of her society. He then reconciled her and her brother, the king, and stipulated that they should rule jointly.

A festival was now held to celebrate the reconciliation.

Just before it, Caesar's barber—a busy, fussy fellow, who was inquisitive about everything—told Caesar that he had discovered a plot against him, which had been formed by Achillas, a general, and Potheinus. So, at the time of the banquet of reconciliation, Caesar killed Potheinus as he entered the hall. But Achillas escaped to the army and started the war I have mentioned.

Caesar had only a few soldiers with him in this large and powerful city of Alexandria. Soon he was without water, for the enemy dammed up the canals. Then, when the enemy tried to cut off his communications by sea, Caesar had to divert them by burning his own ships; the fire spread to the docks and even destroyed the great library. A serious moment occurred when Caesar was engaged near the island of Pharos, the central part of Alexandria. He had to leap from the mole into a small boat to help some soldiers in danger; then, as he was pressed by the Egyptians, he jumped into the sea and swam off. He had a number of manuscripts in his hand and was being shot at and often had to keep his head under water. Nevertheless, he held his hand up the entire time and kept the manuscripts dry. At last, Caesar won, and the king and Achillas disappeared. Thereupon Caesar made Cleopatra Queen of Egypt, but he soon left her; not much later a son was born to her, whom the Alexandrians called Caesarion.

Caesar passed on to Syria and Asia Minor. At Zela, in Pontus, he destroyed Pharnaces, an enemy of Rome, and sent the senate a message that expressed the promptness and rapidity of his action: "I came, I saw, I conquered." The words in Latin all have the same cadence and convey a fine sense of brevity.

There were still adherents of Pompey to put down. In Africa, Caesar had to fight at Thapsus, and also at Utica against Cato the Younger. And in Spain, at Munda and elsewhere, he had to fight against Pompey's sons. His victories, however, brought war at long last to an end. Triumphs, banquets, and other celebrations were held in Rome on a magnificent scale. But a census of the people showed that Rome's population had declined from 320,000 to 150,000. So great a waste had the civil wars made in Rome alone, to say nothing of the other parts of Italy and the provinces.

The Romans, hoping that the government of a single person would give them time to breathe after so many civil wars and calamities, made Caesar dictator for life. This was an out-and-out tyranny, for his power was both absolute and perpetual. But Caesar was moderate and even gave offices to those who had fought against him, such as Brutus and Cassius. He entertained the common people with more feasting and free gifts of grain and founded colonies at Carthage and Corinth, which Rome had destroyed a century earlier. The colonies provided a good place for his soldiers to settle.

Caesar was born to do great things and had a passion for honor. His noble exploits merely inflamed him with a passion to accomplish even more. He now thought of conquering the Parthians and then of marching back— by way of the Caspian Sea, the Caucasus Mountains, and Germany—to Gaul and Italy. He also gave orders to start work on a canal through the Isthmus of Corinth. He planned to straighten out and clean the channel of the River Tiber and to drain the marshes in the neighborhood of Rome, in order to obtain more arable land. Rome's harbor at Ostia was to be improved, too. All these things were merely in the planning stage at the time of his death.

On the other hand, Caesar's reform of the calendar was brought to completion. The calendar was in such confusion that festivals and solemn days for sacrifices were being kept at incorrect seasons. The reform was carried through with great scientific skill, for Caesar called in the best philosophers and mathematicians to work out an exact calendar, one which is still used, as a matter of fact, in my day.

But Caesar's desire to be king brought on him open and mortal hatred and gave the common people their first occasion to quarrel with him. One day, when he was coming down from Alba to Rome, some people boldly saluted him by the name of king; but when he saw that most of the onlookers resented it, he said his name was Caesar, not king. On another day, when a festival was being celebrated in the Forum, Caesar was dressed in his triumphal robe and seated on a golden chair at the speaker's platform, or rostra. Antony, who was then consul, came up to Caesar and offered him a diadem wreathed with laurel. There was a slight shout of approval from the crowd, and when Caesar refused it, there was universal applause. It was offered a second time and again refused, and again all applauded. Caesar, finding that this idea could not succeed, ordered the diadem to be carried into the Capitol.

Such matters made the multitude think of Marcus Brutus, whose paternal ancestor centuries earlier had slain the last of Rome's kings. But the honors and favors he had received from Caesar took the edge off Brutus' desire to overthrow the new monarchy. Those who looked on Brutus to effect the change would put papers near his official chair, with sentences such as, "You are asleep, Brutus," "You are no longer Brutus." Cassius, too, because of a private grudge against Caesar, was eager to be done with him. Caesar had his suspicions of Cassius and once remarked to a friend, "What do you think Cassius is aiming at? I don't like him, he looks so pale." He added that he feared pale, lean fellows, meaning Cassius and Brutus.

Fate, however, is to all appearance more unavoidable than expected. Many strange prodigies and apparitions were now observed. As to the lights in the heavens, the noises heard in the night, and the wild birds which perched in the Forum, these are perhaps not worth noticing in a case as great as this. But, as Caesar was sacrificing, the victim's heart was missing, a very bad omen, since no creature can live without a heart. And it is also said that a seer warned Caesar to watch for a great danger on the Ides of March. When this day arrived, Caesar met the seer as he was going into the senate house and said jokingly to him, "Well, the Ides of March have come." The seer answered calmly, "Yes, they have come, but they are not yet past."

The day before his assassination, Caesar dined with Lepidus. As he was signing some letters at table, the question came up as to what kind of death was best. Caesar answered immediately, "A sudden one." Later, when he was in bed with his wife, all the doors and windows of the house flew open together; he was startled at the noise and the light which broke into their room and sat up in bed. By the light of the moon he could see Calpurnia fast asleep, but he also heard her utter in her dream some indistinct words and inarticulate groans. Later on, she said that she had been dreaming that she was weeping over Caesar, holding him butchered in her arms.

In the morning Calpurnia urged Caesar to postpone the meeting of the senate to another day, but he would not hear of it. After he left his house, a teacher of Greek philosophy, who knew of the conspiracy, slipped Caesar a piece of paper and said, "Read this, Caesar, alone and quickly." Caesar tried to read it, but could not, on account of the crowd pressing in on him. But he kept the note in his hand till he entered the senate.

All these things might happen by chance. But the place that was destined for the scene of the murder—where the senate was then meeting—was the same in which Pompey's statue stood, and had been built by him. A supernatural force seemed to guide affairs to this spot. In fact, just before the murder, Cassius looked at Pompey's statue and silently implored his aid.

When Caesar entered, the senate rose in respect, and then some of the confederates pressed up to him, pretending that they had petitions. As he seated himself, Cimber seized his toga and pulled it down from his neck, which was the signal for the assault. Casca gave him the first cut in the neck, neither a mortal nor a dangerous blow, for he was probably too nervous, here at the beginning. Caesar immediately turned around and seized the dagger and kept hold of it. And both cried out, Caesar in Latin, "Vile Casca, what does this mean?" And Casca, in Greek, to his brother, "Brother, help!"

The conspirators now closed in on Caesar from every side, with their drawn daggers in their hands. No matter which way Caesar turned he was met with blows, he could see weapons leveled at his face and eyes, on all sides he was surrounded by wild beasts. The conspirators had agreed that each of them should make a stab at Caesar and taste of his blood. And so Brutus also stabbed him. When Caesar saw Brutus' dagger, he covered his face with his toga and let himself fall at the foot of the pedestal on which Pompey's statue stood, thus spattering it with his blood. It seemed as if Pompey himself had presided, as it were, over the revenge on his enemy, who lay here at his feet and breathed out his last with twenty-three wounds in his body.

The senators, who had not been part of the conspiracy, now fled out of doors and filled the people with so much alarm that some shut up their houses, and others left their shops. Everyone seemed to run this way and that. Antony and Lepidus, Caesar's most faithful friends, who had been kept out of the senate house during the murder, sneaked off and hid in friends' houses. Brutus and his followers, still hot from their deed, marched in a body from the senate house to the Capitol and called on people, as they passed them, to resume their liberty.

Next day, Brutus and the others came down from the Capitol and addressed the people, who showed by their silence that they pitied Caesar and respected Brutus. Then the senate passed an amnesty for what was past and took steps to reconcile all parties. The senate ordered that Caesar should receive divine honors, and that no act of his was to be revoked. At the same time, it gave Brutus and his followers the command of provinces and other important posts. And so people thought that everything had been brought to a happy conclusion.

But when Caesar's will was opened, and it was found that he had left a considerable legacy to each Roman citizen, and then when his body was carried through the Forum all mangled with wounds, the people could contain themselves no longer. They heaped together a pile of benches, railings, and tables, and then set Caesar's corpse on top and set fire to it all.

Caesar died in his fifty-sixth year, not having survived Pompey by much more than four years. The empire and power which he sought through his life with so much risk, he finally achieved with much difficulty, but he got little from it except glory. But the great Genius, which attended him through his lifetime, even after his death remained as the avenger of his murder, pursuing through every sea and land all those connected with it and allowing none to escape.

The most remarkable of mere human coincidences was that which befell Cassius, who, when he was defeated by Antony and Octavian at Philippi, killed himself with the same dagger which he had used against Caesar; Brutus also committed suicide after that battle. But the most extraordinary supernatural happenings were the great comet, which shone very bright for seven nights after Caesar's death and then disappeared, and the dimness of the sun. The sun remained pale and dull all that year, never really shining at sunrise and not giving much heat. Consequently, the air was damp and the fruits never properly ripened.

CICERO

*(106–43 B.C. Intellectually speaking, the last genera-
tion of the Roman Republic is known as the Age of
Cicero. Marcus Tullius Cicero was antiquity's greatest
orator; he was also a distinguished philosopher and literary critic. He was a defender of the Republic and freedom but, like other men, he occasionally vacillated. The
political strife of the day, the proscriptions and wars,
were enough to try men's souls.)*

It is generally agreed that Cicero's mother, Helvia, was
well born and lived a fair life, but of his father nothing is reported except extreme statements. Some say that
he was a fuller, others that he was descended from Vols-
cian kings. At any rate, the first member of the family
to have the surname Cicero seems to have been worth re-
membering, because his descendants were proud to have
the name, despite its vulgar meaning. For in Latin *cicer*
means vetch, a common fodder; and this early ancestor
had a dent at the tip of his nose which resembled the
opening in a vetch, so people called him *Cicero*.

Cicero, whose life I am writing, replied with spirit to
some friends when they urged him to change his name
on the occasion of his entering politics. He said he would
try to make the name of Cicero more glorious than such

names as Scaurus and Catulus. As a matter of fact, when he was quaestor in Sicily and was offering some silver plate to the gods, he had his two names, Marcus and Tullius, inscribed on it. He told the silversmith that instead of his third name he should engrave the figure of a vetch. So much for his name.

Of his birth, it is reputed that his mother was delivered without pain or labor and that the nurse dreamed that the boy she then suckled would afterward greatly benefit the Roman state. All this might be put down to idle talk, except that Cicero soon proved it true. For as soon as he was old enough to begin his lessons, he showed such talent that the fathers of the other boys would often visit the school to see him. He was renowned for his quickness in learning, but the cruder visitors used to be angry to see their children receive Cicero into their midst with respect. And, since he was eager for every kind of learning, he showed a real weakness for poetry and eventually was known as not only the best orator but also as the best poet in Rome. The glory of his oratory still remains, of course, though his verses have long since been forgotten, since many gifted poets have followed him.

When his youthful studies were over, Cicero then studied under Philon, who was admired for his eloquence, and sought the company of eminent statesmen and senators, from whom he acquired a knowledge of the law. For a short time he served under arms with Sulla, but seeing that political strife was leading the state toward monarchy, he retired to a contemplative life and conversed with learned Greeks.

It was at this time that one of Sulla's emancipated slaves bought up at auction for 2,000 drachmas [1 drachma = 30 cents] an estate of one of the proscribed, who had been put to death. Roscius, the son and heir of the deceased, proved that the estate was worth 250 talents [1 talent = $1,800]. Sulla angrily indicted Roscius for the murder of his father and manufactured evidence to prove it. Not a single pleader before the Roman courts, or advocate, dared take his case, for they all feared Sulla's cruelty. Thus deserted, Roscius came to Cicero and, with the help of friends, persuaded him that he would never have a more honorable introduction to public life. So, Cicero undertook the defense, won the case, and got much renown for it.

But, fearing Sulla, Cicero left for Greece, saying that he was traveling for his health. He was, indeed, lean and light in his build and had such a weak stomach that he could only eat a very little till late in the evening. His voice was loud and good, but harsh and unmodulated; in the heat of speaking he would raise it so high that people feared for his health. When he reached Athens, Cicero studied oratory and philosophy under great teachers. He said that if he should ever be disappointed in his public career, he would leave the Roman Forum for Athens and pass the rest of his life quietly in the study of philosophy.

By the time of Sulla's death, Cicero had strengthened his body by regular exercise and had trained his voice so that it was pleasant to the ear. In order, therefore, to prepare himself better for public affairs and for oratory, which was so important to the statesman, he sailed from Athens to Asia Minor and Rhodes, where he studied both philosophy and oratory. The famous instructor in oratory at Rhodes, Apollonius, did not understand Latin and asked Cicero to declaim in Greek. Cicero complied gladly, thinking that his faults would be more easily pointed out to him, but when he finished, everyone except Apollonius praised him. Apollonius just sat there without saying a word. Finally he said, "You have my admiration, Cicero, and Greece my pity, since the arts and eloquence which are the only glories that remain to her will now be transferred by you to Rome."

On his return to Rome, Cicero steadily rose to first place as an advocate and surpassed others in the Forum. Like Demosthenes, the greatest of the Greek orators, Cicero was at first defective in his delivery and accordingly took lessons with comic and tragic actors. He became very quick in the use of sarcasm, as well as in clever sayings, which was considered effective for a pleader, but he used this technique so much that it offended many and gave him the reputation of having a bad nature. And yet Cicero loved to be praised and was passionately fond of glory throughout his life. Indeed, he won much glory rather early in his life by his successful prosecution of Verres, a disreputable and dishonest provincial governor of Sicily.

Cicero had a very pleasant country home at Arpinum, a farm near Naples and another at Pompeii, but none of them of great value. The dowry of his wife, Terentia, amounted to 100,000 denarii [1 denarius = 30 cents], and he himself had a bequest valued at 90,000 denarii; on these he lived comfortably but simply with the learned Greeks and Romans who were his friends. His house in Rome was near the Palatine Hill, which was conveniently located for those who wished to see him. Actually, just about as many people came to his house as visited Crassus for his riches, or Pompey because of his power. Pompey used to pay court to Cicero, and in return Cicero did much to establish Pompey's authority and reputation in the state.

When he was elected praetor, Cicero managed the courts of justice with distinction. Then both the nobles and the common people joined in advancing him to the consulship. At the time, Pompey was away in Asia, being engaged in war with the kings of Pontus and Armenia. This was the moment chosen by a dangerous individual, Catiline by name, to form a conspiracy against the state. He was a bold, daring and degenerate man, and he attracted the most worthless people in Italy to him. His plan amounted to revolution, no less, with the hope of causing uprisings in Cisalpine Gaul, Etruria, and Rome itself.

This was the famous conspiracy which Cicero had to uncover and thwart during his consulship. Many of the conspirators were debtors, others were former soldiers of Sulla, fierce fellows who dreamed of plundering the hoarded riches of Italy. It was planned to murder Cicero and other officials. On an appointed night one hundred of the conspirators intended to set as many fires in Rome, so that the entire city might all at once be engulfed in flames. At the critical moment, however, Cicero convened the senate, unfolded the long story and then arrested most of the conspirators.

When Cicero returned home that evening from the Forum, the people greeted him along the streets with prolonged applause. Torches and lamps were set up at the doors of houses so that he could be seen better. Many acknowledged that the Roman people were indebted to various generals for the riches, spoils, and power of the time; yet to Cicero alone they owed the safety and security of them, by delivering the state from so great a danger. Not much later Catiline was killed in battle. And then Cato the Younger, in an address extolling Cicero, caused him to be declared the Father of his Country, the first time this title had ever been given anyone.

Affairs did not quiet down in Rome, however. Crassus, Pompey, and Julius Caesar were striving for supreme power. Clodius—the contemptible demagogue, who got himself into Caesar's house one night, when the women were celebrating a religious festival—did all he could to hound Cicero, the defender of law and freedom. Finally, Cicero was exiled, but not much later the people recalled him with tremendous enthusiasm.

Back again in Rome, Cicero was appointed governor of the province of Cilicia, in Asia Minor. He set sail with 12,000 infantry and 2,600 cavalry. There had been many disorders in that part of the world, especially since the Parthians were still a threat. By his mild government Cicero restored confidence and order. He never accepted any of the presents, which were really bribes, offered by neighboring kings; he did away with the charges for public entertainments; and at his own home he received local individuals of accomplishment. His house had no porter, nor did anyone ever find him sleeping in bed, but early every morning he stood in front of his door to receive visitors. He never ordered anyone in his province to be beaten with rods, nor did he ever angrily use arrogant language. When his term as governor was completed, he left for Rhodes and Athens, where he longed to renew his old studies. He did visit the eminent men of learning and saw his former friends. Then, having received various honors, he left Greece for Rome.

Everything at Rome was now, as it were, breaking out into a flame, ready for civil war. Cicero did his best to reconcile Caesar and Pompey, but when Caesar crossed the Rubicon, Cicero decided to withdraw and follow Pompey. However, on account of his health, he was not present at the battle at Pharsalus, where Caesar overwhelmed Pompey. When, finally, Caesar returned to Italy, Cicero advanced to greet him, naturally not without some fear as to how he would be received. But as soon as Caesar saw him, he came forward and saluted him, and ever afterward treated him with honor and respect.

Since the Roman government was now changed by Caesar into a monarchy, Cicero withdrew from public affairs and spent his time instructing young men in philosophy. He set himself to translating various Greek philosophical works. Most of the time he spent at Tusculum, his country seat, and rarely went into Rome. One of his plans was to write a history of Rome, combining it with that of Greece, but he was interrupted by various misfortunes, for most of which he himself was at fault.

For example, he divorced his wife, Terentia, on the ground that she had neglected him during the civil war and had heaped up a mountain of debts. Terentia denied all this and said that the reason for the divorce obviously was Cicero's passion for a young girl of great beauty. On the other hand, Cicero's emancipated slave, Tiro, says that Cicero married the girl for her money. Antony reproached Cicero for putting away a wife with whom he had lived to old age, adding a few sarcastic remarks about Cicero's unsoldierly habits. Antony said this in answer to Cicero's Philippics—for that was the name applied to his bitter orations against Antony, recalling Demosthenes' speeches against Philip of Macedon. Not much later Cicero's daughter, Tullia, died in childbirth, and Cicero divorced his new wife because she seemed to be pleased.

Cicero had no share in the plot that was forming to assassinate Caesar, although he was a close friend of Brutus. After the murder, however, Antony was able to rouse the people to great fury by showing Caesar's dead body in the Forum, together with his bloody clothes pierced by dagger thrusts. Cicero was alarmed for his own safety, but at this moment Caesar's grandnephew and heir, Octavian, came to Rome. He and Antony had a falling out, and thus Cicero and Octavian were drawn to each other. Then fortune took a curious turn, Antony and Octavian were reconciled and, together with Lepidus, divided the Roman government between them, just as if it had been a piece of property. Thus united, they made up a list of more than 200 persons who were to be put to death. There was a long argument about Cicero, but Antony would agree to absolutely nothing, unless Cicero were the first man to be killed. Finally this was agreed to, Lepidus at the same time getting permission to murder his brother, and Octavian his uncle. And so their anger and fury deprived them of their humanity and demonstrated that no beast is more savage than man when possessed with power added to his rage.

While these things were going on, Cicero was with his

brother Quintus at his country house near Tusculum. When they heard of the proscriptions, they decided to make for the coast and sail to Greece. Each of the brothers was carried in his own litter, but they discovered they had only slight provisions for the journey. So Cicero continued on, and Quintus returned home for supplies. Here he was found by those sent in search of him and was slain with his young son.

Cicero embarked on a vessel, but, changing his mind, landed at a point down the coast where he had a house. While he was being carried in his litter, the assassins caught up with him, led by the centurion, Herennius. When Cicero saw Herennius and the others running after him, he told his servants to put the litter down. Stroking his chin with his left hand, as he so often did, he looked steadfastly at his murderers; his own body was covered with dust, his beard and hair were untrimmed, and his face was lined with his troubles. Nonetheless, he stretched out his neck from the litter, and Herennius cut off his head. By Antony's command, he also cut off his hand, with which he had written his Philippics. Thus Cicero died in his sixty-fourth year.

When Cicero's head and hand were brought to Rome, Antony ordered them to be fastened up over the rostra in the Forum, where the orators stand. The Roman people shuddered to behold such a sight and believed they saw there, not the face of Cicero, but the image of Antony's own soul.

After Octavian defeated Antony at the battle of Actium, he made Cicero's son his colleague in the consulship. During that consulship, the senate took down all the statues of Antony and decreed that no one in that family should ever again bear his first name, Marcus. Thus the final acts of the punishment of Antony were, by the divine powers, devolved upon the family of Cicero.

I have been told that a long time afterward Octavian —now called Emperor Augustus by the Romans—was visiting a grandson and found him with a book of Cicero's in his hand. The boy was frightened and tried to hide it under his gown. But the emperor took the book from him and, glancing through a large part of it while he stood there, gave it back to him with the words, "My boy, this was a learned man and a lover of his country."

COMPARISON OF
DEMOSTHENES AND CICERO

(In this volume, the biography of Demosthenes has been placed immediately before that of Alexander, because the lives of the two men, and the issues before them, were so intimately interwoven. In his Life of Demosthenes, *however, Plutarch says that he is making a comparison of Demosthenes and Cicero, a natural enough thing for him to do, since each was the greatest orator produced by his people. Plutarch's comparison is now placed here to give an idea of his method, for it was the general rule of his* Parallel Lives—*where he paired an outstanding Greek with a similar Roman—to conclude each pair with a comparison.)*

Although I omit an exact comparison of the oratorical abilities of Demosthenes and Cicero, nevertheless this much can be said. Demosthenes, in order to make himself a master of oratory, applied all his natural and acquired faculties, so that in the force of his eloquence he surpassed all his contemporaries, both before the political assemblies and the law courts; the grandeur and majesty, no less than the accuracy and skill, of his orations were supreme. Cicero was highly educated, and by diligent study also made himself a master; in his philosophical essays, as well as in his political and judicial speeches, he constantly tried to show his learning.

The different nature of these two men can also be seen in their speeches. Demosthenes' oratory was without jesting and was composed for its serious effect. Cicero loved to mock and would laugh away grave arguments by facetious remarks, if he thought this would aid his clients. He was by nature a pleasant man and generally appeared with a smiling countenance. But Demosthenes continually thought about his expression and usually seemed serious, so that his enemies called him morose and ill-mannered.

If Demosthenes ever touched on his own praises, it was always decently done. But Cicero was forever boasting about himself and would say that arms should give place to the toga, and the soldier's laurel to the tongue. Both men did have the power to persuade people, so that generals of armies needed their assistance. Demosthenes, of course, never held any high office in government, though Cicero did and, at a time when bribery and corruption were rife, he steered an honorable course. Demosthenes, on the other hand, was open to bribery. It was for this that he was exiled, whereas Cicero's banishment was brought about by his ridding the state of villains.

Cicero, however, spent his exile idly. Demosthenes, for his part, went to the cities of Greece and urged them to expel the Macedonians. After his return to Athens, he entered public service again and continued to oppose Antipater and the Macedonians.

Finally, Cicero's death excites our pity, for here was an old man, carried up and down by his servants, hiding from death which, in any case, was so near at hand, and then at the end he was murdered. Demosthenes demands our admiration, for he first prepared poison and then used it. When the temple of the god no longer afforded him a sanctuary, he took refuge, as it were, at a mightier altar, freeing himself from arms and soldiers, and laughing to scorn the cruelty of Antipater.

ANTONY

(ca. 83–30 B.C. History, including Shakespeare, has made famous Mark Antony's passion for Cleopatra, the Macedonian Queen of Egypt. His life brought to an end the century-long revolution which destroyed the Roman Republic. At the battle of Actium, off the northwest coast of Greece in 31 B.C., Antony and Cleopatra were defeated by Julius Caesar's grandnephew, Octavian, who, as Augustus, became Rome's first emperor and introduced Rome's extraordinary era of solid peace and widespread prosperity that lasted 250 years.)

Antony had a noble appearance; his beard was full, his forehead large, and his nose aquiline, giving him altogether a bold, masculine look that reminded people of portraits of Hercules. Indeed, an ancient tradition claimed that the Antonys were actually descended from Hercules. In public he wore his tunic low about the hips, and he had a sword at his side.

Some people found the way Antony boasted and drank in public offensive, nor did they like his eating with the common soldiers, actually taking the food off their tables, but the army, of course, delighted in it. He also helped his friends in their love affairs and took other people's jokes about his own with good humor. He was always

147

extraordinarily generous with his friends and soldiers; this helped him on the way to power and maintained him, after he had become great, when a thousand follies threatened to ruin him.

Antony fought on Julius Caesar's side at the battle of Pharsalus and was in many ways honored by him. But some of Antony's actions caused him to lose favor with the people, while the better class of men found his general course of life, as Cicero puts it, absolutely odious. Utter disgust was excited by his drinking bouts at all hours, his wild expenses, his gross love affairs, the days spent in sleeping or walking off his debauches, the nights at banquets and theaters, his celebrations of the wedding of some comedian or buffoon. Once he drank all night at the wedding of a comedian and then in the morning, when he had to address the people, he came forward, full as he was, and vomited in front of everybody, one of his friends holding his toga out for him.

But Julius Caesar dealt leniently with Antony and cured him of a good deal of his extravagance. As his wife, Antony chose Fulvia, the widow of the infamous demagogue Clodius. This woman was not born to be a housewife but to command generals. So, in a way, Cleopatra was under obligations to Fulvia for having taught Antony to be a good servant.

After Caesar's murder, Brutus and the other conspirators left Rome, while Caesar's friends joined up with Antony. Among them was the young Octavian, Caesar's

niece's son and, by testament, his heir. But Antony re-
buffed Octavian, so the young man attached himself to
Cicero and all those who hated Antony. At this time
Cicero was the most influential man in Rome and persuaded the senate to declare Antony a public enemy. In
the battle that followed, at Mutina in northern Italy,
Octavian was victorious.

Antony and Octavian, however, saw that it was to
their mutual advantage to be reconciled. Accordingly,
they met with another Roman general, Lepidus by name,
and divided the Roman Empire among themselves as if
it had been their paternal inheritance. They had some
trouble agreeing on whom to put to death, each desiring
to destroy his enemies and save his friends. In the end,
hatred of enemies won out over affection for friends. Octavian sacrificed Cicero to Antony, Antony gave up his
uncle, and Lepidus got permission to murder his brother.
I do not believe anything ever took place more truly savage or barbarous than this.

To complete the reconciliation, Octavian married
Clodia, the daughter of Fulvia, Antony's wife. Then
Antony ordered those who were to kill Cicero to cut off
his head and right hand, with which he had written his
invectives against him. When they were brought to him,
he regarded them joyfully and said they were to be hung
up before the speaker's platform in the Forum. In this
way he thought he could insult the dead, while in fact
he only showed his own wanton arrogance and his un-

worthiness to hold the power that fortune had given him.

After their victory over Brutus and Cassius at Philippi, Octavian returned to Rome. Antony went to Greece and amused himself. But he was also moderate and won the reputation of being a Philhellene and a lover of Athens. For there was much simplicity in his character. He was slow to see his faults, but when he did see them, he repented and asked forgiveness of those he had injured.

Such being Antony's nature, the last and crowning mischief that could befall him came in his love for Cleopatra. It awakened in him passions that still lay dormant and kindled them to fury, at the same time destroying his sound judgment. This is the way he fell into the snare.

When he was preparing for the war against Parthia, Antony sent orders to Cleopatra to appear before him in Tarsus in Asia Minor and answer the charge that she had recently aided Cassius. Antony sent his message by a fellow named Dellius. When Dellius got to Alexandria in Egypt and saw the queen's face and noticed her cleverness and her subtlety in speech, he was convinced that Antony would not dream of harming a woman such as this; on the contrary, she would become the first in his favor. So Dellius advised Cleopatra to go (as Homer might express it) "in her best attire" and told her she had nothing to fear from Antony, who was the gentlest and kindest of soldiers.

Cleopatra had some faith in his words, but more in her own attractions. Formerly she had won over Julius Caesar and one of Pompey's sons, and she was sure she would be even more successful with Antony. For she had attracted those other men when she was still a girl, young and ignorant of the world. Now she would meet Antony at the time of a woman's life when her beauty is most splendid and her intellect fully matured. So she prepared for the journey and got together money and gifts and ornaments, worthy of the ancient and wealthy Egyptian kingdom; but her surest hopes were in her own magic arts and charms.

Cleopatra ignored various letters from Antony. At last, as if in mockery of them, she came leisurely to Tarsus and sailed up the River Cydnus in a barge that had a gilded stern and sails of purple. The oars were silver and beat time to the music of flutes and pipes and lutes. She herself lay under a canopy of gold cloth, dressed as Venus in a picture, with beautiful young boys, like Cupids in a painting, standing on each side of her and fanning her. Her maids were dressed like Nereïds and Graces. The boat was full of perfumes which now spread to the shore. Such a multitude of people had run out of the city to see the sight that finally Antony was left all alone in the market place sitting on his tribunal. Word spread among the multitude, as they followed the galley up the river, that Venus had come to feast with Bacchus for the common good of Asia.

On Cleopatra's arrival, Antony invited her to supper, but she thought it more fitting that he should come to her. So, to show his courtesy, he went. He found her preparations magnificent beyond description, but he was most struck by the large numbers of lights. For example, all of a sudden branches were lowered with lights ingeniously placed among them, some in squares and some in circles; it was a spectacle that has seldom been equaled for beauty.

The next day Antony invited Cleopatra to supper. He was eager to outdo her in magnificence, but he knew he could not and spoke to her jestingly of his lack of wit and his rustic awkwardness. She noticed that his jokes were broad and gross, more like those of a soldier than a courtier, and, accordingly, she replied in the same vein. There was no reserve of any kind on her part. For her actual physical beauty, it is said, was not in itself so remarkable that none could be compared with her; rather, it was her presence, if you lived with her, that was irresistible. The attraction of her person, joined with the charm of her conversation and the way she said and did everything, was bewitching. It was a pleasure just to hear the sound of her voice. She could easily go from one language to another and could speak in their own tongue with Ethiopians, Troglodytes, Hebrews, Arabs, Syrians, Medes, Parthians, and others. She had learned the language of them all, which was the more surprising, since most of her royal ancestors had hardly given themselves the trouble of learning the Egyptian language; indeed, several of them had given up their native Macedonian, which was a Greek dialect, and spoke only Greek.

At this time the Parthians had made the son of Labienus—that famous general who had deserted Caesar for Pompey—their commander in chief and were gathered in Mesopotamia ready to invade Syria. And in Rome Fulvia, Antony's wife, was supporting him even with force of arms against Octavian.

Despite all this, Antony was so captivated by Cleopatra that he allowed himself to be carried away by her to Alexandria. There he took a holiday, like a boy, fooling away that most costly of all valuables, time. They formed a sort of company and called it the Order of the Inimitable Livers. The members entertained one another daily, in turn, with an extravagance that beggars description. At this time there was a student, by the name of Philotas, studying medicine in Alexandria. He used to tell my grandfather, Lamprias, that, since he happened to know one of the royal cooks, he was once invited by him to come along and see the sumptuous preparations for supper. When he was taken into the kitchen, he admired the prodigious variety of things; and seeing eight wild boars roasting whole, he said, "You must be expecting a large number of guests." The cook laughed at his utter simplicity and said that not more than a dozen were coming to supper, but that every dish had to be served up just roasted to a turn, and that if anything was but one minute ill-timed, it was spoiled. "And," he said, "maybe Antony will have his supper now, maybe later, maybe he will call for wine, or begin to talk, and will put it off. So, it is not one but many suppers that must be prepared, as it is impossible to guess the hour."

Plato, it will be remembered, speaks of four sorts of flattery, but Cleopatra had a thousand. If Antony was serious or playful, she always had a new delight or charm to meet his wishes. She never let him escape her day or night. She played dice with him, drank with him, hunted with him and watched him do his military exercises. At night she would go rambling with him through the streets of Alexandria; they would disturb people at their doors and windows. Cleopatra would be dressed like a servant, Antony also; sometimes they would come back from these expeditions roundly cursed and even beaten, though most people guessed who they were. The Alexandrians liked it all well enough and said they were much obliged to Antony for acting his tragic parts in Rome and saving his comedy for them.

It would be trifling to tell about all of Antony's follies, but certainly his fishing must not be forgotten. One day he went out fishing with Cleopatra and, not being able to catch anything, he secretly ordered his men to dive under the water and put fishes, that had already been caught, on his hooks. Then he would haul them in. Cleopatra feigned great admiration and told everybody

what a fine fisherman Antony was and told them to come
the next day and watch him. So, when a lot of them had
gathered in their boats, she told one of her servants, as
soon as Antony dropped his hook in the water, to fix a
salted fish from the Black Sea on it. When Antony felt
the pressure on his line, he pulled it in and, as can be
imagined, much laughter followed. Then Cleopatra said,
"Leave the fishing rod, General, to us poor sovereigns of
Egypt; your game is cities, provinces, and kingdoms."

While Antony was thus playing like a boy, two dis-
patches reached him: one from Rome to the effect that
his brother and his wife, Fulvia, had fled from Italy,
having lost in war against Octavian; the other had little
better news, for it said that Labienus, at the head of the
Parthians, was overrunning Asia from the Euphrates to
Syria and Asia Minor. So, at last, Antony roused himself from his debauches and shook off the effect of wine.
He set out to attack the Parthians and got as far as Phoenicia, where he received pitiable letters from Fulvia. Antony, therefore, turned toward Italy with 200 ships, but
on the way he learned from various friends that Fulvia
had been the sole cause of the war with Octavian. She
had hoped that upheavals in Italy would force Antony
to leave Cleopatra. Then, as luck would have it, Fulvia
died in Greece, on her way to join Antony.

This made it easier for Antony and Octavian to patch
up their quarrel. Fulvia was blamed for everything.

When they met in Italy and were reconciled, Antony and Octavian divided the Roman Empire between them, taking as the boundary the Ionian Sea [just where the Adriatic joins the Mediterranean]. Africa was left to Lepidus. They agreed, too, that they should make their friends consuls as they wished, whenever they themselves did not desire the office.

To make the tie even closer, Octavian gave his sister, Octavia, in marriage to Antony, who had been a widower since Fulvia's death. Antony had not given up his passion for Cleopatra, but his reason told him to oppose the charms of the Egyptian.

When finally Antony left Italy for Greece, he brought Octavia along with him, for she had recently borne him a daughter. In Athens he received news that his extraordinarily able general, Ventidius, had defeated the Parthians in battle. Further disagreements with Octavian, however, brought Antony back to Italy once more. Octavia, who had already had a second daugher and was again pregnant, accompanied him. Another reconciliation followed, and then Antony, leaving in Octavian's charge his wife and children and the children he had had by Fulvia, left for Asia.

But that mischief that had long been quiet—his passion for Cleopatra—broke out into a flame as he approached Syria. So he sent word to her to join him. On her arrival he boldly made her a present of Phoenicia, Hollow Syria, Cyprus, much of Cilicia, part of Judea and

Arabia. Nothing so stung the Romans as the shame of this. They were further displeased when he publicly acknowledged as his own the two children he had by her, giving them the names of Alexander and Cleopatra and adding, as their surnames, the titles of Sun and Moon. But Antony, who always knew how to put a good color on the most dishonest action, now said that the greatness of the Roman Empire consisted more in giving than in taking kingdoms, and that the way to carry noble blood through the world was by begetting in every place a new line of kings. His own ancestor, he said, had thus been born of Hercules, and Hercules had not limited his hopes of progeny to a single woman.

The activities of Phraates, the King of Parthia, soon roused Antony to action. Accordingly, he sent Cleopatra back to Egypt, and marched through Arabia and Armenia. When his forces were gathered together, he had for the war 60,000 Roman infantry, 10,000 cavalry, and about 30,000 allied infantry and cavalry. These tremendous preparations alarmed even the Indians and made all Asia shake with fear. But they were useless to Antony because of Cleopatra. For, in order to spend the winter with her, he began the war too early; nor was proper consideration given to the many details.

Antony's haste to finish the war was so great that he actually left behind the engines of war that were absolutely necessary for any siege. They followed along after him in 300 wagons, including a ram eighty feet long.

If these were damaged, they could not be replaced, for this part of the world did not produce trees long or hard enough for such uses.

The battles that followed with the Parthians favored now this side, now the other. But Antony was far from his base; famine threatened, and winter's freezing cold was just ahead. Hardships for the Romans, as well as sudden death, treachery, and ambush, became daily routine, but the famed discipline of the Roman soldier stood, even when Antony made bad military decisions. The retreat was very difficult, however. When at last they got back to Armenia, a land of plenty, the soldiers ate so much that they developed dropsy and dysentery. On reviewing his army, Antony found that he had lost 20,000 infantry and 4,000 cavalry, of whom more than half had perished by disease. In Phoenicia Cleopatra met him with supplies and money.

But in Rome Octavia, desiring to see Antony, asked Octavian's permission to go to him. He granted it, not so much to gratify his sister as to obtain a pretense for war if she were received dishonorably. She no sooner arrived in Athens than Antony wrote her of his new expedition against the King of Media and desired her to await him there. She was much displeased, for she was not ignorant of Antony's real reason, but nevertheless she wrote and asked him where to send the things she had brought him. For she had brought clothes for his sol-

diers, baggage, cattle, money, presents for his friends
and officers, and 2,000 well-armed soldiers.

Cleopatra, feeling that her rival was near at hand, was
seized with fear and feigned to be dying for love of Antony. She reduced her body by a light diet; whenever he
entered the room, she fixed her eyes upon him in a rap-
ture, and when he left, she seemed to half faint away.
She took care that he should see her in tears, and then,
when he noticed it, she hastily dried them and turned
away, as if it were her wish that he should know nothing
of it. Her friends furthered her design, pointing out to
Antony that Octavia had married him merely because it
was convenient for the affairs of her brother. They so
melted Antony that he put off his Median war and went
back to Alexandria.

When Octavia returned to Rome, Octavian decided
that she had been scornfully treated and commanded her
to leave the house of her husband. But she remained in
Antony's house as if he were at home in it and took care
of their children and those he had had by Fulvia. She also
entertained friends of Antony who came to Rome seek-
ing favors from her brother. Thus, without meaning to,
she damaged Antony's reputation, for the wrong he had
done to such a woman made him hated.

Antony also made himself unpopular with the Romans
by a theatrical piece of insolence which he arranged at
Alexandria, and which seemed to show his contempt for

his country. He gathered a crowd together in the gymnasium and caused two golden thrones to be placed on a platform of silver, one for himself and the other for Cleopatra; at their feet were lower thrones for their children. He then proclaimed Cleopatra Queen of Egypt, Cyprus, Libya, and Hollow Syria; he made joint ruler with her, Caesarion, the reputed son of Julius Caesar, who had left Cleopatra pregnant. His own sons by Cleopatra were to have the title of King of Kings. To Alexander he gave Armenia and Media, with Parthia, as soon as it was conquered; to Ptolemy he gave Phoenicia, Syria and Cilicia. Alexander was presented to the people in Median costume, with tiara, Ptolemy in Macedonian, like the successors of Alexander the Great. Cleopatra herself was dressed in the costume of the goddess Isis and gave audience to the people under the name of the New Isis.

Octavian related these things to the senate and people and inflamed men's minds against Antony. Antony therefore now prepared to defend himself and went to Ephesus in Asia Minor with Cleopatra. Ships came in from all quarters to form his navy. He had 800 vessels (including merchant ships), of which Cleopatra furnished 200. She also gave him 20,000 talents [1 talent = $1,800] and supplies for the whole army during the war. They then sailed to Samos, an island in the Aegean Sea.

Kings, princes and governors, nations and cities, had been ordered to bring war supplies. And all the actors that could be found were brought to Samos. Thus, while pretty nearly the whole world was filled with groans and lamentations, this one island for days resounded with piping and harping; theaters filled, and choruses played. Every city sent an ox as its contribution to the sacrifices, and the kings competed to see who could put on the most magnificent feasts. Men began to ask themselves what would be done to celebrate the victory, in view of all the festivities at the opening of the war. Then Antony and Cleopatra proceeded to Athens to receive more honors and celebrate further.

The speed and extent of Antony's preparations alarmed Octavian, who feared he might be forced to fight the decisive battle that summer. The truth is, he lacked many necessaries, and the people hated to pay the taxes required for them. It is commonly agreed that one of Antony's gravest mistakes was not to press the war then and there. Instead, he allowed Octavian time to make his preparations. When these were ready, Octavian declared war on Cleopatra and deprived Antony of the authority which he had surrendered to a woman.

Various prodigies are said to have announced the war. A town which Antony had founded on the Adriatic Sea was swallowed up by an earthquake. Sweat ran from the marble statue of Antony at Alba for days, though it was frequently wiped off. When Antony himself was in the city of Patras, the temple of Hercules was struck by lightning; and at Athens a violent wind threw a statue

of Dionysus across a square. Antony claimed a connec-
tion with both these deities. And then there was a most
inauspicious omen in Cleopatra's admiral's ship, which
was called the *Antonias*. Some swallows had built their
nests in the stern, but other swallows came, beat the
first ones away, and destroyed their nests.

When the armaments gathered for the war, Antony
had no less than 500 ships, including numerous galleys of
eight and ten banks of oars, richly ornamented as if they
were meant for a triumph. He had 100,000 infantry and
12,000 cavalry. Many vassal kings with their own troops
attended on him. Octavian had 250 ships of war, 80,000
infantry and about as many cavalry as the enemy.

So wholly was Antony now the mere appendage to
the person of Cleopatra that, although he was superior
to the enemy in infantry, yet, to please his mistress, he
wished the victory to be gained by sea. And that, too,
though he could see that his captains, for lack of sailors, were pressing into service every description of men
throughout unhappy Greece—mere travelers, mule-driv-
ers, harvest laborers, and boys. Even so, the vessels did
not have their full complement of crews, but remained,
most of them, ill-manned and badly rowed. Octavian,
however, had ships that were built not for size or show,
but for war; not pompous galleys, but light, swift, and
perfectly manned ships.

The opposing fleets gathered off the coast of Greece
at Actium. Canidius, Antony's excellent general, advised

that Cleopatra should be sent back to Egypt and that the issue should be decided by a land battle. But for Cleopatra's sake, Antony would not hear of it.

On the day of the sea battle Antony commanded the right wing with Publicola. Other officers commanded the left wing and center. Octavian put his left wing in charge of Agrippa, and commanded the right himself. The armies were drawn up in order along the shore, Canidius commanding for Antony, Taurus for Octavian. Antony then went in a small boat from one ship to another, encouraging his men.

About noon a breeze sprang up, and Antony's left wing began to advance. Octavian was delighted to see this and ordered his right wing to retire, so that he could entice the enemy out to sea as far as possible. He then planned to sail round and round them with his swift ships and attack the huge vessels of the enemy, which could not be easily maneuvered for their size and lack of men. When they engaged, there was no charging or striking of one ship by another, because Antony's were too bulky to make the blow effective, and Octavian's ships dared not charge head on because Antony's ships were armed with spikes of bronze. Accordingly, the engagement resembled the attack and defense of a fortified place; for there were always three or four vessels of Octavian's around one of Antony's, pressing them with spears, javelins, poles, and fire. Antony's men used catapults to pour down missiles from wooden towers.

While the battle was still equal and the fortune of the day not yet decided, Cleopatra's ships were seen suddenly hoisting sail and making out to sea in full flight, right through the ships that were engaged. Here it was that Antony proved to all the world that he was no longer actuated by the motives of a commander or a man, or indeed by his own judgment at all, and that what was once said as a jest—that the soul of a lover lives in someone else's body—was a serious truth. For, as if he had been born part of her and must move with her wherever she went, as soon as he saw her ships sailing away, he abandoned all those who were fighting and dying for him and followed her.

When Cleopatra saw Antony following her, she gave the signal to come aboard. But as soon as he was taken on, he went forward by himself and sat alone in the ship's prow, without saying a word and covering his face with his hands. They stopped briefly in southern Greece, where he received news of the rout of his fleet. His land forces, however, reportedly stood firm, and accordingly he sent word to Canidius to march speedily into Asia. Actually, however, all of Antony's forces, both by land and by sea, had surrendered to Octavian, and Canidius himself had fled.

Octavian sailed to Athens and distributed what remained of the grain that Antony had collected for his army from the various cities. The cities of Greece were in a miserable condition, having been robbed of their money, their slaves, their horses and cattle. My great-grandfather Nicarchus used to tell how all the people of our little city of Chaeronea had been forced to carry grain on their shoulders down to the seashore, while Antony's men stood by and whipped them.

When Antony reached Libya, he sent Cleopatra on to Egypt and soon joined her in Alexandria. Canidius, his general, arrived with the news of the army's loss at Actium; also that Herod of Judea had deserted to Octavian, as had other kings and princes. None of this seemed to disturb Antony but, as if he were glad to put away all hope, so that he might also be rid of all care, he took up his residence with Cleopatra in the palace and set the whole city into a course of feasting and drinking. Antony and Cleopatra disbanded the Order of Inimitable Livers and put another in its place, just as luxurious and splendid, and called it the Diers Together. Those who said they would die with Antony and Cleopatra handed in their names and passed their time in all manner of pleasures.

Cleopatra now busied herself making a collection of poisonous drugs and, in order to see which of them were the least painful, she tried them out on prisoners condemned to die. She found that the quick poisons always worked with sharp pains and that the less painful ones were slow. Finally she satisfied herself that nothing was comparable to the bite of the asp—a small and venomous horned viper—which brought on drowsiness without any convulsion; the senses were slowly stupefied, so that a person, when bitten by an asp, had no pain but fell into a deep sleep, as it were.

At the same time, Antony and Cleopatra sent ambassadors to Octavian, Cleopatra asking for the kingdom of Egypt for her children, Antony for permission to live as a private man in Egypt or, at the least, in Athens. Octavian would not listen to Antony's proposals, but said that there was no reasonable favor that Cleopatra might not expect.

Cleopatra had built next to the temple of Isis several high and beautiful tombs and monuments. She now brought there much of her treasure—gold, silver, pearls, ebony, ivory, cinnamon and, in addition, some wood and cloth. Octavian, when he reached Egypt, began to fear that in desperation Cleopatra would set fire to all these treasures, and therefore he kept sending her assurances of his good intentions.

Antony, however, thought that he should fight Octavian again, but one contingent of his troops after another deserted to Octavian. He then suspected that Cleopatra had betrayed him. So, fearing that he might do her harm, she fled to her tomb, locked the doors, and sent messengers to Antony that she was dead. In his grief he cried out, "It distresses me that so great a general should have less courage than a woman," and then he ordered his faithful slave to kill him. But the slave killed himself instead, whereupon Antony seized his sword and ran it through his belly. The wound was not immediately mortal, however, and when Cleopatra heard of it, she gave orders for him to be carried to her tomb.

When Antony was brought to the tomb, Cleopatra would not open the doors, but let down ropes from a window. In this way, she and the two women with her pulled Antony up. Those that were present say that nothing was ever more sad than this spectacle; here was Antony, all covered with blood and on the point of dying, holding his hands out to Cleopatra, while she and her attendants pulled with all their strength to bring him up. When they had got him up, Cleopatra placed him on the bed and, tearing off her clothes, spread them over him. She beat her breasts with her hands, lacerated herself and disfigured her face with the blood from Antony's wound; she called him her lord, her husband, her emperor. Antony did his best to stop her lamentations and told her that, of all Octavian's friends, she could rely on Proculeius, and that she should not pity himself, for he had not fallen ignobly but was a Roman by a Roman overcome.

Just as Antony breathed his last, this Proculeius arrived from Octavian. Octavian had been saddened by the news of Antony, but he hoped above all else to get Cleopatra into his power alive. That is why he sent Proculeius to her, but she would not put herself in his power and merely conferred with him through the locked doors. She demanded that her kingdom be given to her children, and he told her to trust Octavian in everything.

Next time, Octavian sent another person to confer with Cleopatra, and while they were talking through the locked doors, Proculeius put scaling ladders to the window through which the women had pulled Antony. It was in this way that Cleopatra was captured. Octavian issued the strictest orders to keep her alive, so that she might grace his triumph in Rome.

Octavian gave Cleopatra permission to bury Antony. She did it with all the magnificence available to her, but she so inflamed her breasts by beating them in her sorrow that she fell into a fever and hoped that she might die. A few days later Octavian came to visit and comfort her. She lay undressed on her bed, and when he entered, she sprang up, having nothing on but the one garment next to her body. She now flung herself at his feet, her hair and face looking wild and disfigured, her voice quivering, and her eyes sunk in her head. The marks from the blows she had given herself were visible on her bosom, and altogether her whole person seemed as afflicted as her soul. But, for all this, her old charm and the boldness of her youthful beauty had not entirely left her. Octavian told her to lie down, and then he seated himself beside her. First she tried to justify her actions, but as Octavian refuted her point by point, she changed and said all she hoped now was to prolong her life. Octavian was pleased to hear her talk this way, being convinced that she desired to live. And so, telling her that his treatment of her would be honorable, he went away, satisfied that he had deceived her, but in fact was himself deceived.

With Octavian's permission, Cleopatra went to Antony's tomb, poured libations on it and lamented bitterly their fate. Then she returned to her tomb, where she was living, took a bath, had a sumptuous meal and lay down. At this moment a country fellow came with a little basket. The guards asked what was in it, and the fellow pushed the leaves aside and showed them that it was full of large figs. He offered them one, but they refused and, suspecting nothing, told him he might enter. Cleopatra then sent Octavian a sealed letter and, putting everybody out of the tomb except her two women, shut the doors. When Octavian read the letter, with its pathetic prayers that she be allowed to be buried in the same tomb with Antony, he guessed what had happened and sent messengers to find out.

The thing had been quickly done. When the messengers arrived, they found the guards suspecting nothing, but on opening the doors, they saw Cleopatra dead, lying on a bed of gold, decked out with all her royal ornaments. Her two women lay dying at her feet.

Some relate that an asp had been brought in among those figs and that Cleopatra, when she saw it, said, "So here it is," and held out her bare arm to be bitten. Others say that the asp had been kept in a vase, and that Cleopatra pricked it with a golden spindle till it seized her arm. But what really took place is not known, and it is even said that she carried poison in a hollow comb, hidden in her hair. And yet there was not so much as a spot found on her body nor any symptom of poison, nor was the asp seen within the tomb; only something like the trail of it was said to have been noticed in the sand, on the side of the tomb which faced the sea. Some say that two faint puncture marks were found on Cleopatra's arm. That is why Octavian, in his Roman triumph, carried a figure of Cleopatra with an asp clinging to her.

Octavian was disappointed by her death and yet admired the greatness of her spirit and ordered that her body should be buried with Antony in royal splendor and magnificence. Cleopatra had lived thirty-nine years, during twenty-two of which she had reigned as queen, and for fourteen had been Antony's partner in her empire. Antony was fifty-three or fifty-six years old on his death.

Antony left by his wives seven children, only one of whom, the eldest, was put to death by Octavian. Octavia brought the others up. They all made distinguished marriages, and from them came three of Rome's emperors: Caligula, Claudius, and Nero. Nero was emperor in my time and put his mother to death, and with his madness and folly came close to ruining the Roman Empire, being Antony's descendant in the fifth generation.